Adventures of a Young Preacher in Salt Lake City

Dr. Charles A. Crane
2020

Adventures of a Young Preacher in Salt Lake City
is available at special quantity discounts for bulk purchase
for sales promotions, premiums, fund-raising, and educational
needs.

For details write
Endurance Press, 577 N Cardigan Ave, Star ID 83669.
Visit Endurance Press' website at *www.endurancepress.com*

The Adventures of a Young Preacher in Salt Lake City

PUBLISHED BY ENDURANCE PRESS
577 N Cardigan Ave
Star, ID 83669 U.S.A.

All views expressed within are the view of the author and
do not necessarily reflect the views of the publisher.

© Dr. Charles A. Crane 2020
All rights reserved. Except for brief excerpts for review purposes,
no part of this book may be
reproduced or used in any form without
prior written permission from the publisher.
ISBN 978-1-7335503-9-0

Cover Design by Janet Colburn

"Scripture quotations are from the ESV® Bible (The Holy Bible,
English Standard Version®), copyright © 2001 by Crossway,
a publishing ministry of Good News Publishers. Used by
permission. All rights reserved."

L.C.
Printed in the U.S.A.

Contents

A Word of Caution 7
Preaching the Gospel often Misunderstood 7
Adventures of a Young Preacher in Salt Lake City 11
    God works in strange ways His wonders to perform
    Salt Lake City, Utah
    The Restoration Movement comes to Utah
Leaving Oregon 15
    A warm welcome awaits us
    The parsonage burns
    Homeless in Utah
    A new meaning to Christian hospitality
    Not so warm a welcome from the LDS
Background for Utah Ministry 21
Next Door Neighbors 23
    The Beckers
    Time to get acquainted with the town you minister in
    The Judge
    The Beckers' long-range plans
The First Day in the Pulpit 27
    Ralph and Margaret Hafer
    Ed and Jean Rollins
The Excommunication Trial 31
    Not so popular with the local Ward leaders
Jerald and Sandra Tanner and Modern
    Microfilm Company 35
Dr. Edwin Hayden 37
    Invited to speak at the North American Christian Convention
    The Keynote Speaker
    Asked to serve on the Planning Committee for the
    North American Christian Convention
    The National Missionary Convention

It Takes Wind to Fly a Kite 41
Invitation from Boise Bible College 45
   Henry Leeper
   Henry fixes the plumbing
   Henry goes hunting
The Bishop's Daughter 49
   Back at the church building
A Sermon at the Post Office 51
My Preacher Won't Baptize Me 53
A College President Comes to Visit 57
   Erskine E. Scates
   The Navajo Christian Mission
   Lunch Break
   The service center
   The first baptism
   Navajo and Shona Tribes
Intermountain Church Planters 63
   The 1967 Camaro
Did God Actually Help Me with My Golf Game? 69
Unique and Wonderful Fellowship 73
   Fast pitch softball
   After-church potlucks
   Halloween and Christmas parties
The Growing Congregation 77
   The early members
   The congregation grows
George Allsbury 87
   George's nephew Sid Allsbury
   A neighboring church
Back in Salt Lake City 91
   The Abels
A Strange Phone Call at the Office 95
   Looking at the Bible

    Looking at the Book of Mormon
    Looking at the Doctrine and Covenants
    King over what and whom?
    Black skin as a sign of wickedness???

At the Senior Dean's Home 101
Grandpa Sleeps in Church 103
Breakfast with the Prophet 105
Another LDS Apostle's Children 109
Sure Would Love to Do That 111
    Tour leader David
    Tour leader Ned
    Safwat Sadek
Church Building Too Small 117
    How is that fastened to your head?
Roy, Utah Church Plant 119
    Murl Jones
    Neal Whittaker
    Harry Ropp
    Dennis Whisler
Are Some of Our Members Polygamists? 123
    The Ladies' Home Journal
    Carol the Polygamist
    Seven Wives
Trouble in Zion 129
Did You Really Say That? 131
Intermountain Bible College 133
Ralph Hafer, a Brief History 137
    Four New Testament Churches
Dr. Max Ward Randall 145
    Dr. Wayne Shaw, Academic Dean
Back in Salt Lake City 147
Looking Back and Looking Ahead 149
    The Church's varied influence

An Introduction

A Word of Caution

The events that I write about in this book are as I remember them. Any inaccuracies in the stories are a result of these events having transpired nearly 50 years ago. Occasionally, I have taken some liberties with the narrative. I believe that the conversations or events are basically as told, but may vary some; but I have sought to accurately represent what took place and to capture the spirit of the events. The stories are all true and told as happened as best I recall. I have changed some of the names out of concern over privacy and that many of the people have since passed on to glory.

Preaching the Gospel Is Often Misunderstood

In the first book I pointed out that preachers are often given a bum rap and are pictured as some sort of necessary but insignificant person in society. They are sometimes shown as sort of dim-witted, sanctimonious, rigid people who pass religious judgment on normal people.

The chief of police in our small town in Douglas County, Oregon said to me once, "Why is such a smart young man like you wasting your life being a preacher?" Although not often spoken, this view is not uncommon.

Is this view of preachers and preaching in touch with reality? No! God had only one son, Jesus, and He was a preacher. Jesus was not a singer, sports star, or politician. His life changed the history of the world and humans' eternal destinies. Most preachers positively impact people's lives and eternities.

Yes, some preachers are lazy and do not offer much of lasting value to the church or society. But this could be said of most professions. This book seeks to examine the true value of the hard-working, godly preacher. In Salt Lake City the young preacher is still learning his craft and makes mistakes, but is well intentioned.

There are three major professions that are basic to the health and well-being of society. First, there is the teacher, who trains the mind and teaches things of value for life. They basically fill the mind with useful tools. Education fills the head with things that make life much more productive and often happier. Those who accomplish the most generally have the best tools in their head. One can dig a ditch with a shovel, but a backhoe adds productivity, so with a proper education that fills the mind with useful tools. Yes, teaching is super important.

A second very important profession is medicine. The doctors, nurses and medical profession help us to be physically well. Without good health life becomes a disaster. We all recognize how important the teaching and medical professions are.

But when reasoning about the value of various professions, the third ministry is often relegated to an insignificant place in our society. Often parents would much prefer their children to become teachers or doctors than preachers. When time to pay a living wage, teaching and medicine usually come out way ahead of those who chose ministry. Is this wise thinking?

Teachers and doctors invest their lives in people's physical lives and in the end lose every patron to death. In reality, without the work of the ministers of Christ, their lives have little lasting value. Don't misunderstand me—I am not suggesting their work is not important; they are vastly important and especially if coupled with the highest calling and profession, the ministry of the Gospel of Christ.

People's lives without Christ in them always end in disaster. People's lives with Christ in them ultimately always end in victory.

Yes, all lives have rainy days, sickness, and tragic events. So what are the values of the minister's work?

First, they are teachers of the Word of God—the Bible. What are those values? I explained to Chief of Police Crumwell (not his real name), that preachers are teachers of morality, honesty, unselfishness, decency, love, hard work, ethics, how to have workable and happy marriages, how to be good parents, and the list could go on and on.

I went on to explain that wherever the gospel has gone, education has followed. Where Christ goes, medicine has followed. Where ever the church goes, freedom and prosperity seem to follow. Observe North and South Korea. South Korea is one of the most Christian nations in the East, while North Korea is mainly godless. One is prosperous the other can't even feed themselves.

I explained to the Chief that the preacher's work brings healing to broken lives. Where else can healing be found for the sinner, depressed, drug addict, liar, drunkard, and again the list goes on and on? Where is better help found for the suffering than the Lord? Without the gospel, society falls apart and ends up in chaos, wars, and death. Where else do we go to lay the brokenness of our lives to rest and begin anew with a clean bill of health?

I asked him where else can the terminally ill turn for a real solution to their soon demise? Where else is there help beyond the grave? All of us are terminal! Yes, the church and godly preachers are the lighthouses for society in every community. Still today there is only one empty tomb. Preachers help people to live in hope and be prepared for their eventual death, resurrection, and eternity.

Without a doubt, the preaching ministry is the most important of all worthwhile professions. It is the profession that truly has an eternal future to it. Following are a few examples of how God worked in the life of a young preacher in Salt Lake City, impacting people's lives for good, and redirecting their lives to usefulness, and a sure and positive eternity. No other profession excels in the opportunity to impact society and lives for good in this life and for all of eternity.

The Adventures of a Young Preacher In Salt Lake City, Utah

Having been ordained to ministry April 4, 1962, the call came to go to Salt Lake City to begin ministry there on January 1, 1966. This seemed rather daunting. Frankly, I felt beset on every side! I was now 27 years old with a wife and three small children, the youngest just over a year old. The events prompting our move had begun a few weeks earlier.

God Works in Strange Ways His Wonders to Perform

Few preachers had ever worked harder than I had during the 3.5 years in the small Douglas County, Oregon, church. I had painted the parsonage and church building. I had mowed the lawns, watered, and weeded them. I had done extensive work on the parsonage and the church building. I did all the janitorial work, including cleaning the restrooms. I had even built a baptistery in the church building that is still in use today.

I had taught Sunday school Sunday morning and Youth meetings in the evenings. I had preached twice most Lord's days. I had taught a class each Wednesdays.

The church attendance had grown from about 60 to regularly 225. There had been 69 baptisms and 33 transfers of membership. The church finances were strong and mission giving was good. I had called on nearly every house in the community to talk to them about the Lord.

Can you imagine my consternation when one of the main leaders of the church took me aside and said, "You have shot your wad and it is time to move on." He cited a failure or two of my family, but having never ever been fired from a position before, I was devastated. To the best of my knowledge, I had lived in clear conscience as the preacher. I went to God in prayer and decided I needed the advice of a mature preacher.

Roy Steadman was the minister of a larger church in Cottage Grove, Oregon and I called and asked if I could come and visit with him. He welcomed me and the next day I sat in his office.

He listened to my tale of woe and then rather cheerfully said, "God must have his hand in all of this—let me explain. A few days ago a friend, Robert Thomas, in Salt Lake City, Utah, called me to enlist my help in finding them a full-time preacher. You just may be the person God has chosen for this task."

Well, it was true that I had led many LDS people to know the real Jesus. The first had been Homer Moxley, and then George Graves and his family of four children. I had also worked with Larry Jonas while in college to confront and teach Mormons. We were reputed to be the "Mormon Experts" and were called upon by Portland, Oregon, area churches to come to their aid when the missionaries "came calling" on their members.

In Douglas County we were having a strong witness in the little town where the LDS were trying to establish a Ward. They failed at that time to plant this Ward. We had ended up baptizing most of the ones they were trying to evangelize. The LDS missionaries returned to Utah discouraged. God almost certainly was directing our lives by what I saw as failure. Tragedy in your life may mean God is working for some future good.

A couple of weeks after talking with Roy Steadman I was on the Greyhound bus heading to Salt Lake City to try out for the pulpit. Mind you, there was only the one man suggesting we leave Douglas County. Later he apologized, saying he had been wrong in suggesting it, but it turned out it was really the hand of God at work. The vote to call the Cranes to Utah was nearly if not unanimous. I returned home to resign and we began our move the first of January 1966.

Salt Lake City, Utah

Driving the U-Haul truck into Salt Lake City, we were overwhelmed by where we had ended up. At first I felt totally inadequate to the task there in the shadow of the Mormon Temple, Temple Square, and the monolithic Mormon Empire.

In addition, the whole area was so large and spectacular. To the east were the towering Wasatch Mountains reaching to the sky over 13,000 feet high. Several large canyons ran back into the mountains: Immigration Canyon, Big and Little Cottonwood Canyons, with Mount Olympus towering over the city, with a huge area of the city called Olympus Bench. This whole area was a majestic place by any standard. The city itself was huge.

To the west was the Great Salt Lake, stretching off to the western horizon. I learned that this lake had no outlet and thus had a mineral content of 27%, second only to the Dead Sea in Israel in salinity. Waters flowing into it came from Utah Lake via the Jordan River as well as the Weber River, Big and Little Cottonwood creeks and many other smaller streams that feed into Salt Lake.

Just south of Great Salt Lake was the Oquirrh range of mountains where the largest open pit copper mine in the world was. It was owned and operated by Kennecott Copper Corporation. The mine was so deep that the Empire State Building could be set in it and one would still look down hundreds of feet to see the top of the building.

The city was at a high elevation of 4250 feet. It was desert with an annual precipitation of 9-12 inches, mostly in the form of snow. There are four distinct seasons of the year. It could be very hot in the summer and very cold in the winter. Weather could be quite unpredictable as on one Fourth of July it snowed on our picnic up Big Cottonwood Canyon. One January we had 76 inches of snow.

The city had been laid out by Brigham Young and since he had the advantage of seeing large Eastern cities, he profited by knowing their mistakes. He made a place for Temple Square and laid out the city reaching east, west, north and south in a grid from the Temple. There were seven blocks per mile and very wide streets. State Street stretched south in a straight line for 30 miles, said to be the longest straight main street in America.

Since the city was in a grid, it was simple to find any desired location by just knowing the address. For example the address might be 1900 S. 2300 E. Maps were unnecessary. Yes, it was impressive and intimidating to this lone, young, and inexperienced preacher of the Gospel of Christ Jesus. To go to a small church plant that had never had a full time preacher was frightening.

The Restoration Movement Comes to Utah

The small church in Utah was the first non-denominational, independent, Christian Church in the State of Utah. There were about 42 members, a parsonage, and a new church building that was in the process of being built. It was indebted for more than its appraised value. They insisted that if we would come, that by faith this dream could become a reality.

There were many different denominational churches there, including the Catholic Church, and even a Jewish Synagogue. Few of these churches were doing much more than just surviving. When they gained new members these members' goal was to move away from Utah as soon as possible, since in reality the State was controlled by the LDS church.

Leaving Oregon

Our pay in Douglas County had been so small ($220 monthly, of which $100 was spent on car expense to do church work) that I had to find a co-signer to help me borrow $650 to pay off my debts before leaving Oregon. The Utah church paid for a U-Haul truck to move our things.

We loaded our belongings and were to leave right after church Sunday morning. The congregation gathered around us and we all cried and they prayed for us. It was worse for us than a funeral. We were devastated to leave those we had served and loved so much.

We headed over the Cascade Mountains in a snow storm with Margaret driving our car and me driving the truck. She cried most of the way over the mountain from fear of driving in the snow. I had put snow tires on the car to make it safer for her to drive in the snow.

A Warm Welcome Awaited Us

The church welcomed us with open arms and helped us move our things into what had been a small farm house on what was now the church property. It sat directly behind the church building. It was quaint, but very charming, with a winding staircase to the upstairs bedrooms. We settled in and began to feel at home.

The church building was only partially completed, but had no floor coverings over the plywood floors upstairs or the concrete floors in the basement. Seating was on Samsonite folding chairs. The building did have heating/air conditioning and an old upright piano.

Parsonage Burns

One week to the day after our arrival, on the first Wednesday evening prayer meeting, as I was teaching a Bible study, and Margaret was at home with a couple of sick children, from the cold weather, and rigors of moving and traveling.

As we were praying, Margaret burst into the meeting in her bathrobe and cried out that "The parsonage is on fire!" I replied, "Where are the children?" She gasped and said, "In the house."

I charged out of the building through about 14 inches of snow and found the house filled with smoke. Gulping my lungs full of air, and running upstairs through the thick smoke, I collected Carol Beth and Doug, carrying them both at once to the front porch to Margaret. Gasping for breath and then running back inside I grabbed Steve out of his downstairs crib. The house was literally burning everywhere.

Margaret then, in a panic, yelled, "Someone get my new piano!" Bob Thomas and I rushed back into the house and grabbed it, carried it out, across the front porch that was covered with snow, down a flight of steps, across the yard, through 14 inches of snow, down another five steps, and into the church basement. We sat it down and he looked at me and said, "Who helped us?" I replied, "Do you see anyone?" He said, "No." We had carried it alone.

This piano was her prized possession. When we first married we had a beautiful 1955 Chevrolet Belair hardtop that was orange and cream color. It was my prized possession. She had wanted a piano so she could practice church music at home. I had sold the Chevy and had taken the money to buy this piano. We still have this piano and I have no idea how Bob and I carried it all by ourselves.

We were now homeless, in Utah, a strange state, the children were sick, and all of our things were covered with burned smoke smell and with dirt and ash all over everything.

What caused the fire? The kitchen range would not work and one of the men of the church was trying to repair it, but he did not know that someone had put pennies under all of the old screw in fuses in the electric box. He managed to short out the 220 volt range and it literally lit up all of the old tube and post wiring throughout the house and set it on fire everywhere.

Homeless in Utah

All of our possessions, including all of our clothes, were nearly ruined by the electrical fire smoke. We had no place to launder things as our washer and dryer were still in the burned-out house and we had no money to do so anyway. The children were sick and Steve was just a baby. My question was, "Now what, Lord?"

A New Meaning for Christian Hospitality

One lady in the church, Doris Monroe, who was at the prayer meeting, said we could come and live a few days with her. There were the two of them, husband and wife, and the five of us in their three-bedroom house. The Monroes were most gracious. (I was surprised when she introduced her neighbors to us, as he was a polygamist with three wives. More will be said about polygamy in Utah later.)

It was clear that we could only stay a few days with the Monroes. Doris' husband was not a Christian but graciously welcomed us. "Where now, Lord?" was my prayer for our young family.

Another family welcomed us into their home, Tom and Ruth Bender. They did not have a very big house, but did have big hearts. They only had a 1900-square-foot, three-bedroom house. There were four of them and five of us. This became our home for the next three-and-a-half months.

We became the closest of friends and one of our evening activities was making banana splits. I finally won this contest with three gallons of ice cream, a dozen bananas, fixed in a huge Tupperware bowl, with all sorts of toppings. After that we all agreed that this had to stop or none of our clothes were going to fit.

After three-and-a-half months, we rented and moved into a vacant house next to the church building. It was owned by a bank. Two weeks later a man showed up at the front door and said, "What are you doing here in my house?" I replied, "We live here." He said, "No you don't, I own this place and you have to get out."

When he bought it the bank had failed to inform him people were living in it. He agreed that all of our things could temporarily be stored in the basement of this house (including the piano) for a few days as he began to paint the inside upstairs. It was back to the Benders, and we began again to hunt for a place to live.

A nice possible house was found for sale down the street and the church trustees decided to buy it, but a congregational vote was needed or the bank would not finance it. That Sunday evening a meeting of the congregation was called. George Abel, our banker, was helping us finance the house. He and his wife will return to the story later.

When the motion was made in the congregational meeting to buy this house, one lady stood up and said, "We can't vote on this yet, we need a couple of weeks to pray about this first!" In shock and exasperation I stood up and said, "Connie, (not her real name) we have been homeless for four months and you have not found time to pray about it yet?" She got up in a rage and stomped out of the meeting crying and my heart sank through the floor. I had really put my foot in my mouth. We are not only homeless, but probably now unemployed.

When I got home to the Bender's house that evening, the phone was ringing and it was Dick, her husband, asking me to come to their house. They were full of apologies and it was all laid to rest without further issue. They became dear friends and workers in the church.

The house was purchased and became our home for several years. It was a fine brick house with a double garage, finer than we had ever expected, much nicer than the old farm house.

Not So Warm a Welcome from the LDS

A Mormon businessman came into my office, (which consisted of a card table and a folding chair) a few days after the fire and said, "I have come to tell you that God does not want you here; why don't you pack up your things and go back to where you came from. This is Zion and you are not welcome here."

I was flabbergasted and replied, "No, you are wrong, that old house was not good enough for a preacher of Christ Jesus and He will give us a much better one." It would be weeks before we were finally settled into the beautiful new parsonage.

Basically we learned that the LDS people were, in many ways, good people. They are solid USA citizens, conservative by nature, hardworking, clean, and with mostly strong families. They make good neighbors. They work hard to convert you to their thinking, which would give us many great opportunities to teach and win them to Christ. During our ministry there, more than 200 LDS people were baptized into Christ. More will be said as we proceed with the story.

Background for Utah Ministry

Mormon Church buildings called "Wards" are kept in near perfect, beautifully maintained condition. Too often Protestant churches are run down and neglected in appearance. This was another way God had been preparing us for ministry in Utah.

While in college, taking my ministerial training, I worked for a tire company called Mike DeCicco and Sons. This tire business was state wide and very busy with a large service shop in Portland, Oregon. I worked there in the service department while attending college, and also worked servicing tires on heavy equipment. I was called "Sheik" by the owners, Mike and Harold DeCicco. Don't laugh, I was then buff and had lots of black curly hair.

A local businessman named Sammy Dardaino owned a car dealership in Portland called "Cadillac Square" and they carried the finest used Cadillacs on the West Coast. We often put new tires on some of his used cars. He soon learned that I loved cars and that I would take extra pains to be careful when installing the tires. He would come in and say to my boss Harold, "I will only let Sheik work on my car." We became friends and he and I always enjoyed each other's company.

One day he said to Harold, "I'm taking Sheik to lunch today." Harold grumbled some, but off we went in one of his fine Cadillacs. At lunch he gave me this lecture. "Charles, you are going to represent the Lord Jesus Christ, you must make the Lord's work look as good as it really is. Nothing succeeds like success and nothing fails like failure."

He explained what he meant, saying, "My parents came from Italy and we were terribly poor when I was a kid. I had to go barefoot all summer because we were so poor. Here is what I have learned that has made it possible for me to become very wealthy and successful."

"As a preacher, you should never appear as a failure. You must make the Lord's work look as good as it really is. You must dress nicely and drive a nice and clean car. The church property must be the nicest in town. There must be no weeds, trash or indications of neglect. Promise me that you will always dress nicely, keep your car, home, and possessions well maintained. You cannot afford to drive an old junker car."

I respected Sammy and have followed his advice. When still back in Douglas County, Oregon, a visiting evangelist flew into our small town to speak at the church, and before landing flew around town. When I picked him up at the airport he said, "The church building's lawns and grounds are the nicest in town," and they were.

In Utah, this good advice from Sammy Dardaino served especially well and the church property and the preacher looked like the gospel was successful. "Nothing succeeds like success, nothing fails like failure. Make the gospel look as good as it really is." This is good advice for any preacher, church, or Christian ministry. Don't go around looking like warmed over poverty, or dressed like a hippie. Hippies may love the Lord and they won't care how you look, but over half of the rest of the population will. The appearance of the church property is the church's most primary advertising.

The Utah church property looked as nice as the LDS Ward buildings or better. One look at the church property and people knew what happened there was deemed important. It represented the creator. The lawns were always mowed and the building spotlessly clean. I dressed like a professional and kept my car clean and polished.

Next Door Neighbors

Next to our new house there were very nice young neighbors. A lady two houses up the street asked if I would be willing to talk to her about their LDS church doctrine.

I agreed, and spent an afternoon studying the Book of Mormon with her. She confessed that for some time she had misgivings about what their church was teaching. She asked if I would come back the next evening and study with her husband, a leader in their Ward (church), the same things that we had talked about.

I brought my book of Mormon and we talked for about two-and-a-half hours. He was amazed when he took a careful look at the Book of Mormon and said he had been completely hoodwinked. He was clearly upset as I left to go home.

His response was to go out and get drunk and he never went back to any church as long as I knew them. I felt like I had hurt more than helped him. I corrected my approach from that point on as to how to teach a Mormon. More will be said about this later.

The Beckers

Another family moved in right next door, Mr. and Mrs. Fred Becker. They had two small children and we had three. He liked nice cars and so did I. He had a beautiful Oldsmobile 442. He was an FBI agent and we soon became good friends. We played board games together and socialized weekly. They began to come to church and the opportunity came to teach them about Christ

Adventures of a Young Preacher in Salt Lake City

and they responded and were baptized.

This led to them introducing us to two other FBI families, both of which became Christians shortly. We remain friends to this day with two of these three families. (We lost track of the third family after they moved.) The other family was Jim and Nona Quick. They have faithfully served the Lord and one son went into Christian ministry.

Time to Get Acquainted with the Town You Minister To

Fred said to me one day, "You need to know more about Salt Lake City where you minister. This evening will you put on a dark suit, white shirt, and dark necktie, so you will look like an FBI agent? We should leave at about 6 P.M."

When we began our survey of town, he first took me to a place where stolen goods were being fenced, that is, marketing stolen goods. The FBI was watching this place to catch them and to shut them down, which the FBI did before long.

We next went to Second South and Second West streets which are about 2-4 blocks from the LDS Temple in downtown Salt Lake City. He pointed out that this was the largest, most open, and active Red Light District in the western states. There were 29 prostitutes working the street that night. He said that often there were more.

One of Fred's duties as an FBI agent was to enforce The Mann Act, which makes it illegal to transport women across state lines for immoral purposes.

Fred said to me, "Want to be solicited?" I replied, "Absolutely not!" He laughed and said, "If we pull over to the curb and roll the window down we will be solicited." I objected to doing this and so instead he suggested that we get out and walk on the sidewalk. This also made me quite anxious. I said to Fred, "Suppose some church member drives by and sees their preacher walking the street in the red light district?"

A beautiful lady dressed in a dark blue suit with yellow trim and matching high heels came up and began to talk with Fred. She had just returned in a car that had let her out near us. Fred asked, "How much did you get for that trick Julie?" She laughed and replied, "Oh, you don't think I would do that for money do you, I do it for love." Well, this is getting pretty risqué so maybe we should change the subject!

The Judge

This was all made possible because the Mormon judge over that area, would throw out any prostitution cases that came before him. He insisted people had the right to do as they wished. I was to learn that often there is a more lax attitude about morality in Utah and that attitude can reach even up to higher levels in the church. It has its foundation in their past Prophets Smith and Young's actions.

As a high school student I had worked for the Stake President of the LDS Wards in our small Oregon town. I became a trusted employee and he would leave me in charge of the truck tire shop when he went out of town for a few days. I was given the keys to his desk where the cash box and receipts were kept. I was shocked to find pictures of naked women there. I had never seen anything like this before. I asked him about this and he said, "Oh, this doesn't displease God, I could have a few concubines, or even several more wives if I wanted, but it is against the laws of the United States and it is really not much different than breaking the speed limit."

This is not to suggest that a majority of LDS people have these attitudes, but this behavior had been practiced and taught as godly behavior by some of their most famous LDS Prophets.

The Beckers' Long-Range Goals

Now back to the Beckers. Fred told me some time later that his long range goal was to be the chief of police of some major city, which did happen a few years later. He became the chief of police of Grand Junction, Colorado.

One day he suggested we should go shooting, which we did. He was the best shot I have ever seen. He could shoot birds on the fly without missing with a 30mm carbine rifle. With a pistol he could crouch and group in the shots in rapid fire at 25 yards. When transferred to Los Angeles he shot a perfect 300 score three years in a row, an almost unheard of feat. No one else had done so for several years. He was an Annie Oakley shot.

Later in his life he became the Warden of the Texas State Prison system and introduced a prison where it was mandatory that the prisoners take regular Bible training. Recidivism came to almost zero in that prison. This prison was so successful that Fred traveled to several foreign countries teaching them how to set up prisons like that. We continue to be friends to this day.

The story about the Beckers is told to illustrate how important the work of Christ really is. A neighbor family became friends and then Christians. Their influence as Christians was widespread across Colorado, Texas, and even to foreign countries. If we plant the gospel seed, then God will make it grow and grow. Few professions offer such possibilities of helping people and even nations as Christian ministry.

The First Day in the Pulpit

The new church building was not finished and that included the parking lot. Because the church had little money, and since they needed fill dirt to level out the parking lot, they had been given free dirt. It had been washed out of gravel and reacted in the parking lot almost like quicksand. The parking lot was a muddy quagmire. It was not even safe to walk on.

That very first Sunday a lady reporter from the Salt Lake Tribune newspaper came to interview me and write an article for the paper about the new preacher. She had been invited by Ralph Hafer, a successful businessman, and member. She came in her new white Chrysler convertible, white dress, and white high heeled shoes.

Of course she drove into the parking lot and immediately mired down to the frame of her car and when getting out of the car sunk into the muck. We were so embarrassed. But a gracious lady member helped her clean up her shoes in the restroom and she did write a nice article about the new young preacher. A couple of men helped get her car out of the mud after church. It was covered in mud.

That week Tom Bender and I ordered several truckloads of gravel and spent several evenings after work hauling 220 tons of gravel, along planks, in wheelbarrows, to dump into the muck, before we got it firmed up enough so one could drive on it and not get stuck. Tom and I had time to work on this together as we were living together in their house.

I began preaching Evangelistic sermons and visiting all the guests who visited church. We passed out brochures, and advertised in the local newspapers. Soon the church began to grow and the next seven years produced 266 baptisms and an additional 460 transfers of membership. About 200 of the baptisms were of LDS people whom we taught and they turned from a fake god to the real Jesus. Many LDS converts were made because the LDS kept trying to win our members. This gave us the opportunity to meet with the Mormon missionaries or Ward teachers. During those years we never lost even one member to the LDS evangelizing efforts.

Ralph & Margaret Hafer

The Sunday that I tried out for the pulpit of the church an old man, he seemed old to me as a kid preacher, said to me, "Come be the preacher and I will become a member and help you." I thanked him and didn't give much thought to it at the moment as I had no idea who or what he was. It turned out that he owned the largest independent truck and auto parts business west of the Mississippi River with over 90 employees at his Salt Lake City business location alone.

He was a tremendous help to the church, and his wife, Margaret, became the matriarch of the church and she was a blessing to all who came in contact with her. Years later she became terminally ill and I traveled back to Utah to visit and pray with her one last time. After our visit and my prayers for her, I asked if she would give me a blessing. She asked that I kneel before her and she placed her old and feeble hands on my head and prayed a wonderful prayer. When she finished she said, "Never worry when you can instead pray."

Ralph taught me many valuable lessons about business. Some of his slogans were, "It takes wind to fly a kite." I asked what that meant and he said, "No business or church can survive without advertising. We must let the whole community know what we are doing here," and we did. He insisted that evangelism was the cure-all for most of the churches' ills.

Another of his sayings was, "Work is too hard to do without having money working for you." I asked what this meant. He replied that physical work can only be done for a few hours each day, but money works 24 hours a day 365 days a year. He said, "You must learn to invest wisely so money can work for you."

He always wanted to travel with me when I was speaking at churches, revivals, working with the Navajo Mission, Intermountain Church Planters, or Intermountain Bible College. This meant that he had a major influence on my life for good, even though his formal education ended in the third grade, due to the death of his mother, father and older brother, leaving him alone at 9 years of age.

More will be said about the Hafers later.

Ed and Jean Rollins

Early on in the ministry in SLC a new family showed up at church and said, "We thought we should attend church here at least once before we are baptized into the LDS church." (This baptism was supposed to happen to them the next week.) "We still have some questions and reservations." I requested that I meet with them Tuesday evening. They agreed if they could also invite the Ward teachers to be present. The time was set for the following Tuesday evening at 6 P.M.

As I thought about this meeting I grew more and more uneasy, not knowing what to expect right here in Zion under the shadow of the mighty church. A fellow preacher, a graduate of Intermountain Bible College, had come to my office a few days before and introduced himself. We became friends immediately. Feeling a bit unsure and knowing Marvin Cowan had been a former LDS and was quite well read, I called and asked if he would assist me. The Rollins agreed that he could come with me.

At the meeting I soon began to feel sorry for the poor LDS teachers, they were totally unprepared for what was taking place. Finally they began to boast about their church being the fastest growing church in the world. Marv said "That is not true, you are losing members constantly and never take anyone off of your church rolls." They said, "We keep our rolls up to date regularly, what you are saying is not true." Marv replied," I left the church 17 years ago and became a Christian and I am still considered a member of the Midvale Third Ward."

Well, the evening ended and Ed, Jean and their son were baptized, not at the Mormon Ward, but at the Christian Church instead. Marv and I gave little more thought about the evening's events until a few weeks later. Marvin called and was concerned since he had been summoned to appear before the Mormon Ward's excommunication council, called the Bishop's Court. He asked that I go as a character witness for him, which I did.

The Excommunication Trial

The night of the excommunication trial there was a judge, witnesses and quite a few people, along with several friends of Marvin and me who were in attendance. When the trial began they asked Marv, "You are a Protestant minister, aren't you?" Marv said, "I plead the fifth amendment." They said, "You are, aren't you?" He sat silently.

Finally out of the silence Marv asked, "You don't have any evidence for this charge against me?" They said, "No." He said, "It is just like your whole religion, built on no evidence. Do you have a phone book?" One was produced and he said, "Just look up my name, and yes, I am a preacher of a Conservative Baptist church."

A bit later it was my turn to speak. LDS people are to be excommunicated mainly for serious social or moral infractions. So I asked, "Are you excommunicating Marvin Cowan because he is not a fine Christian man?" The judge said, "Oh, no." I said "May I ask another question" and I was told that I could. "Is it the LDS church policy to excommunicate fine Christian men?" The audience roared with laughter and Marv was excommunicated and we were promptly and summarily dismissed.

Not So Popular with Local LDS Ward Leaders

One evening a few weeks later when I was returning home from a hospital visit, I recognized the man in the car next to me at a traffic light. He also recognized me as he was one of the LDS men at the excommunication trial for Marvin Cowan. He looked at me angrily and shook his fist at me.

I was driving my 1961 Mercedes 190 D car. Car expense for a preacher is usually a major item, and then diesel was 17 cents a gallon. While out calling on a new family I noticed this car sitting in the family's front yard and it appeared to not be in use. I asked the man if he would consider selling it and he agreed to sell it to me for $300. It had many problems since it had sat without being driven for months.

I towed it home and began work on it. I replaced the brakes and shocks; the differential was leaking grease which I fixed by putting in new seals. I repaired dents in the fenders and fixed the grille that was caved in.

After doing all the body work and painting the repaired parts with primer paint, I took it and had a nice paint job put on it. I added a new set of whitewall tires. It looked very much like it was new and I had about $800 in it. One family complained that I was being paid too much if I could afford a new Mercedes.

A member of the church was chief mechanic at the large Caterpillar dealership. He asked if I could use lots of diesel and I replied I sure could. He would bring me 2–3 barrels of fuel that had been drained out of the huge machines they were repairing. I went for months without buying any fuel.

Well, this diesel car was very efficient but also quite slow. On the evening when the LDS man was glaring at me when the light changed, we started out and he, with his new Mercury, decided to run me into the ditch. He blew his horn and ran me off of the road into the borrow pit between the lanes of the connector.

Fortunately, I was not stuck and was able to follow him home, due to traffic lights that stopped him, and I pulled into his driveway behind him. I got out and walked up to him and he locked his car door, but rolled the window down a bit.

I said to him, "You better hope that my Christian faith is real, for if it isn't I might drag you out of your car and give you the beating you deserve." I then said, "Well, my faith is real and you are safe, but I sort of doubt that your faith is real or you would not be running a Christian minister into the ditch." He looked at me like a deer in the headlights, rolled up his window and I turned and left.

This was the first of several threatening actions and phone calls from LDS people warning that they might just shoot me. Another of the Mormon leaders caught me in a crosswalk and came at me with tires squalling and shaking his fist at me while trying to run me down. I had to dive out of the way to avoid getting hit.

It became clear that all was not well in Zion. The church ruled Salt Lake City and Utah. People are welcomed unless they rock the boat. If you stand up for what you believe and point out the glaring errors of their Empire it can become downright dangerous.

Jerald and Sandra Tanner—Modern Microfilm Company

Marvin Cowan and I became very good friends and he asked if I knew Jerald and Sandra Tanner. I did not, so he suggested that I go to their office and make their acquaintance. I was in for a huge blessing.

Jerald was the nephew of N. Eldon Tanner, one of the Mormon Apostles. Sandra's maiden name was Young and she was a direct descendant of Brigham Young, the Mormon Prophet who became Prophet after Joseph Smith's death. Both had been raised in the LDS church and were of inquiring minds.

During their college days at Brigham Young University they became friends and eventually married. Together they begin to doubt what they were being taught and began to research and examine their churches' teachings and especially old church records and histories.

Because of who they were, they had access to many things non-Mormons did not. It was not long before they discovered that they had been grossly misled and they accepted Christ as their personal saviors and turned from the cultish church in which they had been raised.

Jerald was a quiet and thoughtful man, who was a master researcher, while Sandra was warm and outgoing. Together they made a wonderful team and they provided a lot of very valuable and helpful new insights from their investigations. Few people, if any, have done more to display information about the founding and history of the LDS church. They are probably the most influential of all who have taught about the errors of Mormonism. Some of their books are:

1. *Mormonism—Shadow or Reality*, with over 400 pages and 27 chapters.
2. *3,913 Changes in the Book of Mormon*, a photocopy of the original Book of Mormon with all the changes marked from the original to the modern edition.
3. *Changes in the Doctrine and Covenants*, which compares the original and modern versions with 2,876 changes marked and 21 doctrinal reversals.
4. *Changes in Joseph Smith's History*, 62,000 words have been added or deleted.
5. *Joseph Smith's History*, by his mother, Emma Smith, which the LDS church has thoroughly revised and edited, leaving an inaccurate picture of who Joseph Smith really was. The Tanners have reproduced the accurate and original edition.

The Tanners have produced over 40 books, making available old and rare manuscripts and revealing the convoluted history of the Mormon religion. Without a doubt the Tanners have done more than any other individuals to enlighten the Christian world to the strange and sometimes evil world of the LDS church.

The Tanners' works became a wonderful resource for my study and ministry to the LDS people. At the same time as meeting the Tanners, we had a guest speaker, Edwin Hayden, Editor of *The Christian Standard* magazine, the oldest religious periodical in America.

Dr. Edwin Hayden

Dr. Hayden had called and asked if he might speak at the church (we had been buying copies of *The Christian Standard* for the membership), and of course he was warmly welcomed. It was a great pleasure to have the editor of the nation's oldest Christian Magazine to honor the pulpit of our church by his presence.

It just so happened that there were eleven LDS people, whom we had been teaching, that were scheduled to be baptized that Sunday. When the invitation hymn was sung they all responded to the invitation. Brother Hayden had preached a fine sermon and this added to the excitement of the morning.

Dr. Hayden was quite impressed with the work of the Christian Church in Salt Lake City and wrote a great article for *The Christian Standard*, featuring the church with a picture of the front of the church building and an article giving a glowing report of the church. This picture graced the cover of *The Christian Standard*.

Invited to Speak at the North American Christian Convention

A few weeks after the article appeared in *The Christian Standard* I was invited to hold a workshop about the LDS religion at the North American Christian Convention. This was one of America's largest Christian conventions. I gladly accepted this challenge and took copies of two small books I had written and also huge boxes of the Tanners' books. Some of the books I took were original copies of the Book of Mormon and the Doctrine and Covenants.

The workshop was filled, beyond the capacity of the room, with people anxious to learn about the Latter-day Saints. Some people could not get into the room as it was full to capacity. All of the books were sold and many expressed their appreciation for the information they had received.

It was a great blessing to be with the many thousands of people in attendance, and I was given a booth where people could come by and visit with me and ask questions about the Mormon Church.

The Keynote Speaker

I still remember the keynote speaker and his opening sermon. The preacher was Wayne Smith. He was the preacher of one of the largest Christian churches in America. He read his text and then said, and I will try to quote him as accurately as possible.

Smith said, "My wife said, 'Honey, you can't tell that story at the convention, please promise me that you will not tell that story!"

Wayne, who was rotund, began to laugh, holding his stomach and guffawing loudly.

Wayne then said, "I told the elders of my church the story and they said to me, 'Wayne, you cannot tell that story at the North American, promise us you will not tell that story."

Wayne again begins to laugh again almost uncontrollably and said, "Yes, Yes, I am going to tell the story!"

Wayne then said, "One of our members, a farmer, had a bad tooth and had to go to the dentist to have the tooth pulled. When he got there he told the dentist how afraid he was of having his tooth worked on and the pain. When the dentist was ready to pull the tooth, he got the forceps into his mouth and the farmer bit down on them. He told the farmer that he needed to keep his mouth open wide so he could pull the tooth. On the next try the farmer bit down on his thumb and the dentist had to quit again, rubbing his sore thumb."

Wayne said, "After trying three more times without success, the dentist decided he needed to think more creatively. He knew that his receptionist had long sharp fingernails. He thought, 'I will get her to come in and help me, when I am about to pull the tooth I will have her sink those claws into his rear end,' which she did, and while the farmer's mouth was wide open he yanked out the tooth."

Smith said, "The farmer gurgled a bit, coughed and spit, and then he said to the dentist, 'I had no idea a tooth's roots went that deep.'"

Smith's point was that his roots went deep into scripture, and his theology was founded in and upon Holy Scripture and that is why he believed in restoring biblical Christianity.

Asked to Serve on the Planning Committee of the NACC

My workshop had gone very well and a few months later an invitation came for me to serve on the committee that planned this large convention. I accepted gladly and enjoyed the camaraderie this group of godly men shared. It was a welcomed relief from the constant stress of serving Christ under constant and severe opposition in Utah. I served many years in this position on the Board of Directors of the NACC.

I learned that many of the most famous preachers had a great sense of humor and knew ways it could be expressed. As a whole they are a happy bunch of fine men.

Serving on the Board of the North American Christian Convention made it possible to meet men like Dr. Wayne Shaw, and Leon Appel, President of Lincoln Christian College and Seminary. These are two of the finest men anywhere.

I learned later that President Appel and I were both led to Christ by the same evangelist. This helped forge a special friendship.

Seldom have I had more enjoyable times than with these godly leaders from across America. It was pure pleasure a few years later to become a student under Dr. Wayne Shaw at Lincoln

Christian Seminary, where he was Academic Dean, and where Leon Appel was President.

Not all was fun and games but there was wonderful fellowship with thousands of Christians from across America. There was fantastic music, moving preaching, and hundreds of very useful workshops. The North American Christian Convention has been one of America's greatest religious conventions. Year after year I continued to have workshops there and served on the Board of Directors.

The National Missionary Convention

As a result of the workshops at the NACC, an invitation came to have a similar set of workshops, at the National Missionary Convention about the LDS religion. This would make this material, about the errors of Mormonism, available to church leaders and missionaries from around the world. For several years following I was invited to provide these workshops at both conventions.

It Takes Wind to Fly a Kite

This was one of the lessons Ralph Hafer taught me. Many children have learned this lesson. If there is no wind, a person can run their legs off and the kite will just flutter to the ground. But with a steady wind, kite flying can be lots of fun.

Brother Hafer, our successful auto and truck parts businessman, had said this to me several times before I asked him what he meant by saying it takes wind to fly a kite. He said business and church is like flying a kite. The wind that makes a business or church work is advertising. We must let everyone know what great things are available at the church of Christ. This will require advertising and publicity. From his encouragement the church already had a special listing in the phone book and in the newspaper. These things did produce some results.

As a result of the fine article about the church by Dr. Edwin Hayden in The Christian Standard magazine, I received a letter from a college student at Ozark Christian College in Joplin, Missouri. He requested that he come for his ministry internship for a summer at the church in Salt Lake City.

My thoughts turned to "kite flying." With an energetic college student, preparing for ministry, we just might really increase our outreach by advertising. It would also involve the young people from the church in ministry for Christ. The dream was to have him come to lead our high school youth in passing our 10,000 brochures to houses all over the area of Salt Lake City where the church was.

It was arranged that he come and live with us in the parsonage and we would house and feed him and he would work with the youth, especially in handing out the brochures.

We worked hard to make a very nice brochure that showed the church in its best light. He arrived in Utah and moved into our basement bedroom.

Soon I began to learn about this young man's basic skills, he liked to eat and sleep. It was clear he had not been raised on a ranch like I had, where one was up while it was still dark and worked till after sundown.

The 10,000 brochures were brought to the parsonage and stacked near his bedroom door. I gave him suggestions as to how to proceed and offered to help him recruit his helpers. The work began the first week and several hundred brochures were handed out. I then noticed that instead of getting up and at the task in the morning he was still in bed long after I had gone to work.

After a few weeks I noticed that all of the brochures were gone and heaved a sigh of relief as I had begun to wonder if he would accomplish this task. I got him out of bed one morning before leaving for the office and asked him how it was coming.

His reply still disgusts me, "Brother Crane, do you know how hard it is to pass out 10,000 brochures? It is just too much so I just sent all of them off in the garbage."

I replied, "What! You just threw them away? They cost the church a lot of money."

He said, "Well, it wasn't going to work anyway, everyone here in Utah is LDS and they hate our brochure."

He proved to be almost useless and was sent back to Joplin weeks early. But wind will make a kite fly and also advertising makes the church grow. From the about 300 brochures that were passed out a new family showed up at church and what a family they were.

Mr. and Mrs. Hal and Gay Bryon were new to town and came to church because of a brochure on their door. They were already dedicated Christians. They became members and blessed the church for several years. You see, Hal Bryon was the head of the Food and Drug Administration for all of Utah. They not only worked hard in the church but were responsible for several other families coming into the church family.

Yes, it is true it takes wind to fly a kite. Who knows what the results would have been if all the 10,000 brochures had been handed out. Nevertheless, the church grew dynamically for many other reasons, one of which was that the Gospel of Jesus Christ was proclaimed week after week from the pulpit and in the classes for all ages.

An Invitation from Boise Bible College

The next spring an invitation came for me to speak at the Spring Conference at Boise Bible College. Along with graduation, each spring, people would gather in Boise, Idaho, for a week of workshops and preaching. This was a time for Christians to gather for fellowship and to encourage each other.

Henry Leeper

When we arrived, hospitality was offered to us by Mr. and Mrs. Henry Leeper. Henry was a small German man with a salt-and-pepper mustache and cute German accent. Henry was an elder in the church and owned a service center for German cars, Mercedes, BMWs, Audis, and Volkswagens. His shop was spotlessly clean and in a fine brick building. The garage was on one side of the building facing the street and the same building reached through the block to the other street. The business on the other side, Henry said, was a bank.

Henry Fixes the Plumbing

Henry told us that the plumbing in the garage had plugged up. They had tried all sorts of cures, the plumber's friend, the snake, chemicals, and all without success. One of his employees had come up with the idea that since they had an air compressor with 275 pounds of pressure they might be able to blow out the plugged drain. He suggested that they take the clean out plug that was in the garage floor, put in a large air hose, pack rags around the hose and then cut loose the 275 pounds of air to blow out the clog.

When they had it all set up the employee was standing on the rags and Henry was at the valve on the compressor he was to open. When the employee said, "Hit it" Henry fully opened the valve and they could tell pressure was building up in the plumbing when suddenly there was the sound of things breaking loose.

Through the wall of the bank building they heard a man crying, "Help!, Help!" They went next door to the bank to check what was wrong and found a man still in the men's room all covered with water, crud and filth. The clog had blown up through the toilet that the man was sitting upon. It had lifted him to the ceiling and covered him with filth, but thankfully he was not seriously hurt, but grossly soiled.

Henry, the little German man, with the salt and pepper mustache, commented in his German brogue, "I guess he had a cold water enema." He said the plumbing now works fine, but Henry worried that the man may not again rest easy in the men's room, at least not for a long while.

Henry Goes Hunting

Henry said he loved to hunt. He was back in the woods near Idaho City hunting and was sitting on a stump. He said he was in camouflage dress, with only a small red ribbon tied around the brim of his hat. He was waiting hoping that some deer would come by so he could shoot it and fill his deer tag.

He was sitting quietly when a shot rang out from down the valley and the bullet hit the stump on which he was sitting. He said that he turned and looked but saw no one and so fired a warning shot back down the hill. He heard no more shots and gave no more thought to the occasion.

A few weeks later he was working on a man's fine Mercedes and the fellow told him about being up hunting and almost shooting a man sitting on a stump. The man said he saw movement and thought it was a deer. He said fortunately he was not a very good shot as he had missed his target and his bullet had hit the stump the man was sitting upon.

The man said, the fellow on the stump turned and shot back at me and literally shot the hat off my head!

Needless to say, we enjoyed the Leepers' hospitality and have never forgotten the stories about fixing the plumbing and hunting deer.

The Bishop's Daughter

Instead of Mormon Wards having a preacher, they have a presiding Bishop who serves in many ways similar to what a preacher does. The big difference is that they have no formal training or degrees, but only have cursory and brief training and a plan of leadership that they are to follow. Usually they are ill prepared to fulfil their roles of leadership. Every once in a while one of these Bishops would come and ask advise about how to do something, like how to have a funeral or wedding.

On this occasion, a son of one of our Elders began dating the Bishop's daughter whose last name was also Bishop. By this time I had become well known and so the big guns were enlisted to confront this young pest who was baptizing LDS people. The meeting was set to take place on a Tuesday evening when I was to meet with the LDS teachers and also our Elder's son and the Bishop's daughter.

Another LDS man, Pat Patton, asked to be invited as a silent observer. His wife and daughter had recently been baptized and he was not pleased about it all as he was losing control of his little eternal kingdom and his route to becoming a God.

When the evening came I again was prayed up as I felt anxious that I be open to the Lord's leading and not so nervous as to not think clearly. It was one of those occasions when I opened my mouth and the Holy Spirit gave me the exact words to say, and the evening again left the Ward teachers in total disarray and confusion. The Elder's son's future wife was baptized, as well as Pat Patton, and they all became close and special friends. Pat will return to the story later.

Adventures of a Young Preacher in Salt Lake City

David and Eileen were soon joined in Holy Matrimony by me at the Christian church, and for years he has followed in his father's footsteps by serving as an Elder in an Idaho Christian church. She has raised a fine Christian family and served the church. We remain dear friends.

Back at the Church Building

As previously mentioned, the church building was only partially finished when we began ministering there. None of the flooring had been laid. Tom Bender and I laid all of the squares of tile in the sanctuary and ended up with blisters on our knees from doing so. It was even harder to lay the tile on the basement concrete floor. This is how Tom and I spent our evenings while we lived with them after the parsonage burned.

A crew of members joined together in framing up the classrooms in the basement, sheet rocking, taping and finishing the walls and ceiling. I built dividers on wheels that could be moved around in the large common area to make more spaces for classes to meet as the church continued to grow.

It was not long before the church had enough money to buy church pews, a grand piano, and church organ. Another lot was purchased next to the church property for additional parking and all of the parking was black topped and striped. All of this gave more room, but it was not long before the building had to be doubled in size, extended out over the area where the farm house had been. This enlarged building was also soon too small.

A Sermon at the Post Office

A few weeks after the excommunication trial for Marvin Cowan, I was taking a mailing to our local post office. I was surprised to learn that Nathan, the Judge at Marv's excommunication trial, was the postmaster. He greeted me with some signs of distaste. In turn I greeted him warmly.

Just then another preacher came in, Chuck Taylor, from a nearby new Southern Baptist church plant. We had become acquainted since they had been borrowing our church baptistery, since they did not yet have one. I turned to talk with Chuck when Nathan called out, "Pastor Crane, you don't associate with Southern Baptists, do you?" (This was a very busy post office with a constant stream of people coming in and out. On this occasion no one left, but a small crowd formed to listen.)

I replied in a clear voice, "Of course I do, because I am a Baptist, also Catholic, Methodist, Presbyterian, Episcopalian and Latter Day Saint." This got everyone's attention as things came to a halt, and additional people kept coming in and joining those already listening while I explained.

"You see, Nathan, I believe in baptism by immersion since that is what the Bible teaches, so I am a baptized Baptist believer. I believe the true church includes every Christian, everywhere. The word Catholic means universal. The true church is truly universal or catholic. The church I belong to includes every person ever saved from all time. I am committed to returning to Bible methods which means I am a Bible Methodist. The Bible church is to be led by Elders and Bishops, which means the Bible church

Adventures of a Young Preacher in Salt Lake City

is Episcopal and Presbyterian, since these words mean elder or bishop." I had everyone's attention now while others joined as they came in.

"What might surprise you, Nathan, is that I believe I am a saint of God and that we are now living in the last days, meaning that I am a real Latter Day Saint. But what might surprise all of you is this. I am sick and tired of all of the denominational sectarianism, division, non-biblical practices, and squabbling. I am trying to just return to clear Bible teachings and point people to Jesus and to what is proven to be true. That is why when asked what I am, that I say, 'I am a Christian.'"

"I was shocked, to learn, recently, Nathan, that the LDS church now has seven major splits, and about 100 minor divisions. This just doesn't make sense to me, and I am sure Christ is also unhappy about all this confusion, so I have chosen to be called "Christian" which does not divide me from anyone who loves Jesus as their Lord."

As I left the post office and was at the door, I looked back and Nathan was just standing there shaking his head, looking confused, and the many other people were standing looking like deer in the headlights of a car, watching me as I left.

My Preacher Won't Baptize Me

I was leaving my office one day, not long after, when a new black Lincoln sedan pulled up beside me in the parking lot. The beautiful lady put down the power window and looking out asked me, "Will you baptize me?" (I noticed that she had a huge diamond wedding ring.) I was rather shocked and said, "Wow, I am not used to having people approach me in the parking lot asking to be baptized." I said, "Do you have time to come into the office so we can talk about this?" She said, "Yes" and parking the fine automobile she came into the office.

My first impression was that she was beautiful but full bodied, that is probably weighing 350 plus pounds. I selected a sturdy chair for her as she began to explain her need.

She explained, "I attend the local Methodist church and have been studying the books of Acts and Romans in the New Testament. It seems pretty clear in Acts and Romans people were not sprinkled, but immersed. I have talked with my preacher asking him to baptize me and he has refused, saying they did not have a tank and my being sprinkled as an infant was good enough."

I opened my Bible and together we examined what it says about baptism and this confirmed what she had learned herself. She asked if she could bring her husband and would I baptize her? This we did that evening. She now began to attend church with her son and daughter and they too were baptized. Her husband, Jim, did also attend some. Jim did not become a Christian until several months later.

Adventures of a Young Preacher in Salt Lake City

A few weeks later she asked me if I could use some help with the church office secretarial work. I did need help and she began working as my assistant. She was super qualified and could take shorthand faster than I could talk. She could type so fast that the electric typewriter could not keep up and would get jammed. All of Ruth's work was with near perfection in everything she did.

She soon knew what was going on throughout the church, almost better than I did, and became a valuable source of what was going on behind the scenes. But there remained one serious problem.

Her husband explained to me that when they had married she was not heavy and was thought to be the most beautiful woman in the county. He showed me a picture and he was right. Even as a full-bodied woman she still sort of glowed with personality and intelligence. But, well, let me explain.

It had to do with seating at her desk. The regular desk chair did not last a week. I heard a crash in her office and rushing out found her amidst the wreckage of the chair on the floor. This necessitated me finding a truly sturdy chair for her. It was stronger and lasted a few weeks before she twisted without getting up and another pile of junk was on the floor around her. Fortunately she was not seriously hurt either time.

At the same time Ruth continued to be a soul winner and wonderful help in all she did. I found her pleasant to work with and one person said to me that no one would suspect that she was sitting on my lap. But what was I to do for a chair for her?

I looked around the church building and the strongest chairs we had were Samsonite folding metal chairs. I tried one and it seemed to solve the problem and did for a couple of weeks. Ruth came into my office and sort of embarrassed said, "Charles I ruined another chair." I asked, "What happened?" She said, "I twisted around without getting up and the chair just crunched down."

Yes, the chairs were guaranteed and when I took a trunk load of twisted chairs back to be replaced the dealer said, "These are the only chairs we have ever had ruined, what are you doing to them?" I explained and got a trunk load of new chairs.

A few months later the problem was solved and Ruth and her family moved to Florida. She was seriously missed, a beautiful full bodied saint of God. We remained friends for years until Ruth and her husband's deaths. They had remained faithful Christians and helped lead many others to Christ.

A College President Comes to Visit

Erskine E. Scates

The Salt Lake City church had been founded by Bob and Toni Thomas. They had three children: Angie, Becky, and Daniel. Bob had been transferred to Salt Lake City by the major company he worked for, Hercules Powder Company. He was a mathematician. They were Christians, and finding no biblically sound church near where they lived, had contacted Erskine Scates, President of Intermountain Bible College, in Grand Junction, Colorado, to help them start a church.

He had suggested that they begin a Bible study group in their home, which they did. Soon there were a few other families gathering in their family room each Sunday, singing some hymns, with Bob teaching a lesson, and then all of them taking communion together.

Erskine suggested they could invite one of the professors over to preach for them some and one began to come more or less regularly. Eventually he was hired part time and worked at Mr. Hafer's truck parts store part time. This arrangement continued until some ethical problems forced him to resign. This was when I was hired.

Soon after our arrival Erskine came to visit us, and I immediately was enthralled by this wonderful and godly man. He and his wife, Faith, had five boys and he soon said he considered me a sixth. What a blessing he was to me and the church in Salt Lake City.

Not long after, he had me coming to Grand Junction to teach a few days each semester, primarily in the area of the cults, and especially the LDS religion. In a few months I was elected to the Board of Directors of the college and our small church, with the help of Mr. Hafer, became the number one supporting church for Intermountain Bible College, both of money and students.

While serving at the college, I began to meet his sons, Erskine Jr., David, Harry, and there were two others sons I never had the opportunity to meet. Each of them was a graduate of Intermountain Bible College with advanced degrees from universities. They were all well-educated and eloquent. They were fine, godly, and capable men.

Navajo Christian Mission

David was working as a missionary to the Navajo Nation near Four Corners, where Utah, Colorado, Arizona and New Mexico meet. David asked if I would serve on the Board of the Navajo mission, which I agreed to do. I was on the board for the remainder of ministry in Utah. For two years served as chairman of the board.

It was quite a drive from Salt Lake City to the mission location. We (Mr. Hafer and I) would start early in the morning, driving south on Interstate 15, turning east just south of Provo, across the mountains to Helper, with its coal mines, and then to the small city of Price, that was settled on the east side of the Wasatch mountains.

Leaving Price, we would drive on towards Green River, but before getting there would turn south to Moab. Moab is just south of The Arches National Monument, and not very far east of Dead Horse Point, where one can look out over the Grand Canyon and see the Colorado River way below.

Lunch Break

We would stop for lunch in Moab at JR's Roadkill Restaurant. Their slogan was "You kill it ... we grill it!" They said that "Eating food is more fun, when you know it was on the run!"

Of course all of this was a spoof and actually they had pretty good food. The items suggested on this menu were not actually served. We looked forward to this stop because it was

```
EATING FOOD IS MORE FUN,           CANINE CUISINE
  WHEN YOU KNOW IT WAS
       ON THE RUN!                YOU'LL EAT LIKE A HOG...
         ENTREES                WHEN YOU TASTE YOUR DOG!
                              Slab Of Lab . . . . . . . . . . . . . . . $2.95
Center Line Bovine . . . . . . . . . . . $4.95    Pit Bull Pot Pie. . . . . . . . . . . . . . . . 1.95
"Tastes real good, straight from the hood"         Cocker Cutlets. . . . . . . . . . . . . . . . 3.95
The Chicken . . . . . . . . . . . . . . . 3.95    Shar-Pei Filet. . . . . . . . . . . . . . . . . 5.95
"That didn't cross the road"                      Poodles 'N' Noodles . . . . . . . . . . 5.95
Flat Cat . . . . . . . . . . . . . . . . . . 2.95  Snippet Of Whippet. . . . . . . . . . . 4.50
"Served as a single ...or in a stack"              Collie Hit By A Trolley . . . . . . . . . 3.95
                                                  German Shepherd Pie . . . . . . . . 3.95
A TASTE OF THE WILD SIDE                          Round Of Hound . . . . . . . . . . . 4.25
        (Still in the hide)                       GUESS THAT MESS
Chunk Of Skunk . . . . . . . . . . . . . $1.95       - A Daily Special Treat -
Smidgen Of Pigeon . . . . . . . . . . . 1.95      If you can guess what it is
Road Toad Ala-Mode . . . . . . . . . . 1.65         YOU EAT IT FOR FREE
Shake 'N' Bake Snake . . . . . . . . . . 2.25
Swirl Of Squirrel . . . . . . . . . . . . . 1.55  LATE NIGHT DELIGHT
Whippoorwill on a Grill . . . . . . . . 3.30
Narrow Sparrow . . . . . . . . . . . . . .55     Rack Of Racoon . . . . . . . . . . . . $3.95
Rigor Mortis Tortoise . . . . . . . . . 6.75     Smear Of Deer . . . . . . . . . . . . . . 4.95
                                                 Awesome Possum . . . . . . . . . . . 1.95
         BAG-N-GAG                               Cheap Sheep . . . . . . . . . . . . . . . .49
Our daily take-out Lunch Special!                 Served Fresh Each Night After Dark
```

still a long drive on to our destination. At the reservation there were no restaurants or fast food. It would be a while before we had another meal. In another couple of hours we would arrive at our destination. The board meetings would last all afternoon.

The Service Center

We tried various things to try to break through into the Navajo culture. Since most all of the people lived in hogans, an igloo-type of structure, made of sticks and mud, in which they had no running water, way to bathe, or way to wash their clothes, we reasoned that a Service Center might be a way to gain their friendship and trust. So we built a center, with a good well, clean

Adventures of a Young Preacher in Salt Lake City

running water, washing machines, toilets, and showers for them to use. They did begin to use this center, before long it was quite busy, but they still did not open up to us or to the gospel.

I remember going out with David Scates to visit in their hogan homes. These dome-like structures' only doorway faced east to get the morning sunlight. Inside was a single metal stove in the center with a pipe going out through the center of the roof. These small stoves were made of tin and they used them to cook on, make flat bread right on top of the stove, and to heat their hogans in the cold times of year. There was a chair or two and simple cots to sleep on. Everything was usually covered with dust.

I recall going into one hogan where a woman was nursing a baby. When we left I asked David why grandma was nursing a newborn baby. He explained that was not her grandma, but the mother. She is no more than 30 years old, he told me. I said, but she looks so old and is wrinkled and turning grey. He said that life on the reservation is very tough, especially for a woman.

As already said, many of these hogans are very remote with no water or sewer facilities anywhere near. Water must be brought from miles away, the desert is their bathroom. We did provide a place for them to get water, bathe, and wash their clothes. Their response to our generosity was rather taciturn.

It seldom rained on the desert, but when it did it often came in torrential downpours. This would wash off the mud roofs and damage the mud walls of the hogan. David observed this problem and took sacks of concrete to the next site where they were building a hogan. He poured the sack of cement into the big hole where mud was being mixed to plaster the roof and sides. After this the rain did little or no damage to their hogans. Others soon adopted this practice.

The first two years were painfully fruitless as there seemed no way to break into their culture. The reservation did not have good educational opportunities for children. In a Board meeting someone suggested that we might try taking some of these children into our homes where they could be involved in a Christian home, church, and public school. Salt Lake City was the first to try this and three boys were brought there and lived with three different church families for the school year.

At the next Board meeting we got on our knees in the hogan and prayed for just one Navajo person to come to Christ as a sign that we were supposed to be there trying to evangelize.

The First Baptism

I remember bringing the three boys to Salt Lake City. They came first to our home. They were fascinated with the toilets in our house as they had never used such a thing. They were playing with them, putting their hands in the water, and repeatedly flushing them. We had three toilets, one for each boy to play in. It was amusing to hear the toilets flushing around the house.

At first there were almost insurmountable issues, as everything was new for them, but gradually they began to adapt and learn. The mission still had not had even one conversion or baptism.

It was my honor to baptize the very first convert, David BeGay, in the baptistery at the Salt Lake City church. He grew up to be a godly man and leader among the people of the Navajo Nation as they turned to Christ through the work of the missionaries. David Scates and Vernon Hollett's efforts at evangelism were greatly successful eventually.

In our next meeting we agreed that success came only as a result of prayer. We had prayed for one and David was baptized. We decided to pray for a dozen. But how were we to win these Navajos?

The Board thought that maybe we could have sort of a brush arbor meeting place, near the river, with good music, singing, instruments, and preaching. At the very first one of these meetings when the invitation was given only three responded. So Vernon Hollett said they went to the river to baptize and when they had finished 12 people had been baptized.

This led to prayers for 24, and in the next riverside meeting, more than 30 were baptized. Vernon had been studying the

Navajo language and learning to read and speak it. This led to him reading selected portions of the Bible, in Navajo, on the radio station, that reached all over the reservation. He gave brief messages about the meaning of the passages he had just read.

By then most Navajo families had at least one transistor radio and thousands had the scriptures read to them day by day in their own language. For most it was the only station they could get on their small radios. For many this was their first contact with Christ and Christianity.

A few years later, when Vernon and I were in Grand Junction at the same time, he gave me a tape to play in my car as I drove back from Grand Junction to Salt Lake. While listening to the tape, as I drove, I got to crying so hard I had to pull off of the road. Vernon was saying on the tape, "The Navajos are coming to Christ, thousands are responding to the gospel, and the main religion of the Navajo Nation is now Christ and Christian."

Navajo and Shona Tribes

David Scates learned that the Navajo Indians of the Southwestern States and the Shona Tribes of Southern Africa were very similar in social and administrative structure. He thought that comparing evangelizing methods might help both mission works to be more fruitful.

So David traveled to Kenya and worked with the missionaries there for a few weeks. Unfortunately, while there, he contracted a viral type of cancer and returned home very ill and died within 30 days. I still grieve when I think of the death of this big, strong, and godly man who did so much to turn the Navajo Nation to Christ.

Intermountain Church Planters

With the growth of the Salt Lake City church, many opportunities for ministry materialized. I was asked to serve on the Board of the Intermountain Church Planters Organization. Its headquarters was in Denver, which necessitated my going there twice a year. With my already busy church schedule, this made attending the meetings rather difficult.

One meeting was to take place at 10 A.M. Monday morning in Denver and I was to be in the pulpit Sunday A.M. and P.M. I solicited the aid of a recent convert, Pat Patton, to help me drive, and we left after evening church to drive to Denver. This meant that we would get to Denver in time for me to attend the meeting the next morning, and then in the evening after the meeting, we would return to Salt Lake City. Pat would be able to sleep during the day while I was occupied.

The 1967 Camaro

I had an almost new 1967 Chevrolet Camaro. This probably needs a word of explanation as to how a young and poor preacher could have such a nice car. A busy preacher drives a lot and usually this for me amounted to 45-50,000 miles a year. My 1964 Chevy II Nova was approaching 100,000 miles and was beginning to require frequent repair and service. Each time it was in for repair, I was left sitting at the dealership awaiting its return, while church work was neglected.

You may recall that when leaving Oregon I had to borrow $650 to leave Oregon with all my bills paid. This money was now coming due monthly and I was having to sell Hertel Bibles to earn the money to pay this bill.

Why sell Bibles in Utah? I had learned that often LDS people did not own a Bible, but did have a Book of Mormon. This gave me the opportunity to sell these big and beautiful family Bibles. On Monday, my day off, I would drive to surrounding areas and sell these Bibles door to door. This is how I paid off the borrowed money.

This added to the normal driving and made it even more crucial that I have a dependable car and not be stranded far from home. In desperation I bought a new 1966 Chevy II Nova and it proved to be a piece of junk, broken down every week, for the few months I had it, and I had no car to do the church work.

In desperation I complained to the district sales manager for Chevrolet and he graciously got me into this beautiful new Camaro. It was as trouble free as the Chevy II had been a constant problem. It was this car that Pat and I drove to Denver. He was delighted to drive me and especially with this fine sports car. We expected to have a fun time, two young fellows, in this fine road car.

The trip over was without incident and Monday evening we gassed up the car and headed back home. It was cold winter time and the roads were slick in places from time to time. We had to stop for gas in Green River, Wyoming and for some reason the station attendant checked the radiator and left off the radiator cap. About 20 miles down the road the heater quit working and we were freezing in the car. We stopped and found the problem, at another station, refilled the radiator, and proceeded on our way. It was then well after midnight.

This was before the Interstate had been completed and as we approached Evanston, Wyoming I was sleeping all slid down in the seat with the seat belt fastened up around my chest, exhausted since I had not been to bed since Saturday night and it was now 2 A.M. Tuesday.

A recent snow storm had plastered the road signs with snow so they were unreadable. We were traveling about 65 miles per hour and I felt the car begin to skid, I sat up quickly, leaving the seat belt loose, when we hit a big light pole, went through a chain link fence, took out a small tree, and the car came to rest right next to a house. I was unconscious and bleeding profusely from head wounds.

What had happened was that the unreadable road sign had said there was a 90-degree turn and this turn was covered in a sheet of ice and instead of turning we ran straight ahead at 65 miles per hour into the huge light pole, shaking a large light off of it, tilting the pole over, mashing the car in half way to the windshield, spinning around through the chain link fence, hitting the tree with the rear quarter panel, and bending the rear axle down.

The car was totally demolished. I had hit the door so hard with my shoulder that it was bent outward, there was a metal piece between the front window and car door that was torn off and it cut a swath along the top of my head, my head then took off the front rearview mirror, and I lay bleeding on the broken front passenger seat. The police came shortly and they took us to the hospital in Evanston.

The accident had left me blind and when we got to the hospital about 3 A.M. and I wanted to call my wife, Margaret. Since I couldn't see, I asked the nurse to make the call so I could explain to Margaret what had happened. I explained to the nurse I wanted to talk to her so that it would not worry her.

When Margaret came on the line she said, "Where are you?" I replied, "Really, I have no idea." She asked, "What is going on?" I said, "Well we have had a pretty bad car wreck." She asked, "Were you hurt?" I said, "Yes, I have had a couple of hundred stitches to wounds on my head and I am now blind." The nurse grabbed the phone from me and assured Margaret that I would live but would need to be in the hospital for a while.

What happened to my friend Pat Patton? Pat was a super strong man and he had pushed the steering wheel right down through the dash, broken off the brake and clutch pedals, his arm had flown back hitting his forehead and leaving the pattern of his expandable watch band across his forehead. Otherwise he was not seriously hurt and his wife drove to Evanston the next day to take him home.

In reality my injuries were not terribly serious, a cut from my forehead back across my head requiring a dozen or more stitches, a large ridge across the right side of my head caused by hitting my head on the roof above the passenger door, a seriously bruised arm and shoulder, and blindness caused by a serious concussion.

I was taken back to Salt Lake City and spent the next week in the hospital. In a few days my sight returned when the swelling in my brain subsided.

Again, the young preacher had no car in which to make hospital calls, and for visitation to all the new attenders at church. So while still in the hospital, on the telephone, I purchased another Camaro from Streeter Chevrolet. It was a 1968, red with black vinyl top, fancy wheels, four speed transmission, and it was more beautiful than the previous blue one. It was delivered to me as I was released from the hospital.

Were there any valuable lessons to be learned from all this mess? Probably should have been, one was that it is not smart to not go to bed at night. Another was that it is better to learn to say no than to over extend oneself. Another important lesson is that driving in the winter months, in the mountains of the West, can be dangerous, so don't drive at night.

The Intermountain Church Planters had a part in beginning several new churches, one in Idaho, and two of which were in Utah, along with several others. This trip was not a total loss.

Did God Actually Help Me with my Golf Game?

Two families in the church ran a golf course not far from the church building, out on a street called the Diagonal, near Highland Drive where the church was located. They gave me a set of very nice golf clubs and let me play free, and also gave me some instruction.

Because of such a busy schedule my golfing was spasmodic, and I excelled in various golf shots like the slice, the hook, the water shot, and affection for the rough and the sand traps.

One day while playing with a friend, I hacked a golf ball into some fancy houses near the course and the last I saw of my ball it was ricocheting off of the roofs of mansions. Needless to say I was far from a golf-pro. I used to say, "I often play in the seventies and if warmer than that I stay home." You get the point, I was not much good at golf, but did enjoy trying.

One Sunday a well-dressed man in his mid-forties came into church by himself. As usual, I made an appointment to meet with him that same week. When we sat down together in his apartment he asked me all sorts of leading questions. After I had committed myself on the Bible and many Bible doctrines he just tore into me and criticized most everything I believed. He then said he was an "ordained preacher." He said, "Young man, you have a lot to learn."

I later learned what denomination he was a part of. Even though I left his house wounded and discouraged by his crude and cruel remarks I was gracious and kind to him, believing that one always acts like a gentleman when in someone else's home and so he continued to attend church.

That week after leaving his apartment, I did a little investigating and found out that he had been fired by his church and divorced by his wife for repeated acts of adultery. Our church was a happy place, with good music, and gospel preaching that he seemed to value. No doubt God was at work at the church, using me a young and inadequate preacher.

A few weeks later as he left church he asked if I might join him for a game of golf. I agreed and the time was set for the following Thursday. When he picked me and my clubs up he told me we would be joined by two other players at Mountain View Golf Course, up Immigration Canyon, near Salt Lake City.

As we drove he explained that he was a par golfer, that he belonged to the country club, and was a near professional quality golfer. In keeping with his rather strong personality, he controlled the conversation and said he would coach me and help me become a better golfer. I said, "Please do not do that as it makes me nervous and ruins the game for me."

As we set up at the first tee, he began to criticize everything I was trying to do. Trying to be gracious, I kept my mouth shut and proceeded as I always had. I was more than a bit nervous and bothered by his overbearing ways.

The first hole was a four par. I was shocked when I hit the ball and in two strokes was lying about two feet from the pin and in the hole with a birdie.

As I addressed the next shot, at a three par, he again told me I was doing it all wrong and that I had the wrong club. This time with my seven-iron I put the ball within 18 inches of the pin and again was in with a birdie. Wow, I had never played like this ever before.

The next hole was a five par with an awful distance to go. I addressed the ball with my number one driver and could not believe how far the ball flew and with my second shot landed the ball on the green next to the pin and ended up with an eagle, two under par. Big Mouth had suddenly gotten quiet and I was having a very good time. After nine holes I was well under par and seven strokes below him.

After eighteen holes I was five strokes below him and more than that with others of the foursome. By eighteen he had begun to rail at me and finally said, "You are not only a lousy preacher, but you are also a bald-faced liar about your golf game." He never returned to church and somehow I really didn't miss him.

Thinking back on that day, there was no doubt in my mind that God had been present and saw to it that I was encouraged and a hypocrite preacher was put in his place. Yes, God just kept showing up to help in times of need to help the young preacher in Salt Lake City.

Over the years many times events have transpired in which it is clear that God does bless and direct our lives, if we do what we can to serve Him. So many events in Salt Lake City were directed by God to greatly increase the usefulness of a young and inexperienced preacher. No doubt God had helped me with my golf game that day. Unfortunately He has never helped my golf game again. "To God be the glory" as He surely did help that day as I played golf with the backslidden preacher.

Unique and Wonderful Fellowship

It wasn't long before a strange and lovely trend became apparent in the church. The growing congregation was especially united in love for one another. As I contemplated why this was true, it became more and more apparent why.

Many of the members were from other places and had been transferred to Utah by their companies. Mixed in with these were the LDS converts who had been rejected by their families and shunned. We were a bunch of pilgrims in what was, in fact, a mission field. We did not have extended families anywhere near us, except for the other members of our church. This led to many glorious times of fellowship. Let me mention a few:

Our Fast-Pitch Softball Team

Clyde Benton, one of the elders, loved baseball and knew the game well. He organized our team. I had played fast-pitch softball for years and loved it also. We formed a team and joined a city league. Salt Lake City is a center for this sport. Soon we were playing each week, in the spring and summer. The competition was fierce.

One team we played against had as their pitcher a man who had pitched three World Series of Softball championships. He was awesome. But then we had Tex Christenson, who was a left-handed marvel. I was the catcher and without knowing what pitch he was going to throw, it was very difficult to catch his pitches. His pitching was awesome. His pitches came in so fast that my catching hand was bruised all season.

Then there was Rick Bender on our team. He was not only a great shortstop player, but also a master at stealing bases. Another team member, Pat Pintus, could hit the ball over the outfield fence and over the outfield scoreboard beyond the fence. Then there was lanky Larry Kingsley who could almost rip the cover off of the ball with his home runs.

It was soon an all-church event for us to gather for the weekly, or bi-weekly, softball games. It was a time of sweet fellowship and fun. In five years our team won the championship three times and came in second twice.

One evening we were in the final inning of the championship game and the score was still 0 to 0. I was catching and it was the last out and a runner was on third base. When the ball was hit, the play was at home base and I had the ball. The runner came at me to knock me out of the game, and Tex Christenson, our pitcher, saw what was happening, and met the runner near home base and slugged him in the stomach. Tex, myself, and the runner, were all piled up together near home plate. The runner was out, but we lost the game for poor sportsmanship. It was the ninth inning and the score was still nothing to nothing. Baseball brought us together in sweet fellowship. This was one of the two seasons we came in second.

After-Church Potluck Dinners

Fellowship dinners are often held at the church building, and sometimes this was true for the church, but more often for us they took place at nearby parks and places of beauty. One of these was a campground, up Big Cottonwood Canyon, just a few miles from the church building. One day in particular stands out in my mind.

We had reserved a picnic area near Cottonwood Creek. This was a few miles up the canyon's winding road that at the top came to the Big Cottonwood Canyon Ski Resort. The road was crooked but ran along, and often across, the rushing mountain stream.

The majestic Wasatch Mountains rose to the sky on both sides of the roadway.

A heavy growth of oak-brush covers the mountain and grows right down to the rushing stream. In the spring and summer the small trees are green and in the fall they turn various colors of rust and orange. The mountains are majestic and beautiful all year. This area is of rare beauty.

Cottonwood Creek is fed from the melting snow on the high mountains, and from many fresh water springs that flow strongly all year. The waters of the creek are crystal clear and clean enough to drink. It was a near perfect place for warm Christian fellowship and godly fun.

On this Sunday afternoon, we had cooked hamburgers and hotdogs over an open fire and eaten our potato salad, cakes, pies, and other goodies, when one of the teenagers decided to throw some water from Big Cottonwood creek on another kid. It was a hot summer day and soon we all were involved in a fun time of an all-church water contest. It was done in good fun and fellowship. Before we were finished, a couple of the rascals got re-baptized in the rushing cold water in wholesome fun. We all dried out, because it was a warm summer day, before we went happily home.

Halloween and Christmas Parties

Because of the season these holiday parties took place at the church building. Each Halloween we had all sorts of competitions, such as dunking for apples, and spinning the bottle. We played all sorts of fun board games and the whole church grew in their love for each other. The end result was the church's attitude of loving fellowship.

At Christmas, the party included a music extravaganza and it was customary for gifts to be given by the congregation to the church staff. Margaret and I had just recently purchased our own home, which was not totally finished yet, and I was finishing the lower level of this fine home.

Bob Thomas had the job of presenting Margaret and my gifts. He began by saying, "Never in the history of the church has a church leader been given the privilege of giving such a gift to their preacher. It is a great honor for me to present our preacher and wife these gifts tonight."

A couple of large boxes were carried out by the deacons and set near the pulpit and the audience began to chuckle and laugh. They knew what was in the boxes but Margaret and I had no idea. They had beautiful colored paper and big bows. I opened the first up and it was a toilet! The whole congregation burst into raucous laughter. I sat with this rather foolish look on my face at a loss for words. The other package was a sink.

I was ready to finish the downstairs bathroom and I needed these things to complete the project. We received many special gifts at these annual Christmas parties.

At these gatherings, all sorts of creative and strange games were thought up and played. Needless to say the church was filled with loving and happy

Margaret in front of our house.

Christians. It was no wonder it continued to grow into a thriving and healthy church with people coming to Christ regularly.

The Growing Congregation

The Early Members

When we arrived in Salt Lake City the first of January 1966, there were about forty-two members. Many of these were extraordinary people. We should probably begin with the Thomas family since they started the church in their home.

The Thomases

Robert and Toni had three children: Angie, Daniel and Becky. Bob, as he was called, had been a high school math teacher and now worked for Hercules Powder Company in their business office. He had served in the Navy during the war and after had gone to college and earned his bachelor's and master's degrees. He was a fine and steady Christian man.

Bob and Toni years later.

Bob

He had one issue that he struggled with, and that was that he smoked a pipe and wanted to quit this habit. He and I talked about this and Toni told me that in frustration he had thrown all his smoking gear down over the bank behind their house into the thick oak brush. Bob confessed to me a couple of weeks later that

Adventures of a Young Preacher in Salt Lake City

he had gone down and searched out his stuff from the oak brush and was back smoking again.

A few weeks later Bob came to my church office with a couple of boxes of his smoking things. He told me, "If you have these I will be too embarrassed to come ask you for them and this will help me quit." Reluctantly I put his smoking things in the trunk of my car and took them home. About a week later he came into my office looking pretty discouraged. "Please, can I have my smoking stuff back? It is way too expensive to buy it all again." I went to the house and got his stuff that I had stored in my little shop in the basement.

Bob eventually won the victory over this habit, and during all this time proved that he was truly committed to the work of the church and Lord.

Toni

Bob's wife, Toni, was and still is a rare jewel. She is petite, pretty, charming and well educated, with a degree from the University. Her training is in art and she is an accomplished painter. She, Bob, and their daughter Angie all were gifted singers. Bob sang bass, Toni sang alto, and Angie has a strong soprano voice, and was the delight of the whole church with her glorious solos. What a huge thing the Thomases did for the Lord and church in Salt Lake City.

The Benders

Tom and Ruth Bender had two sons, Tommy and Rick. Tommy, the older one, was shy and almost reclusive, while Rick was outgoing, and both boys were superb athletes. Tom senior was a machinist and worked making parts that were used in Boeing airplanes. He was as fine, wise, and godly a man as could be found anywhere.

Ruth had a strong alto voice, and was often a part of the fine music organized by Margaret. But Ruth's greatest gift was insight into people's personalities and characters. Give her five minutes with a person and she could read who and what they were almost better than they knew themselves. She proved to be an asset as whenever someone new came to the church that I felt uncertain about I would ask Ruth for her evaluation. She was right almost 100% of the time.

We especially loved the Benders due to our living with them for three-and-a-half months when the parsonage burned.

The Benders were a great part of making the church what it became. Unfortunately both Tom and Ruth died young, he of a massive heart attack, and she of cancer.

The Hoopers

Another of the early families that blessed the church was Gordon and Helen Hooper. Gordon worked for Deseret Pharmaceuticals and his job was designing and making the equipment for I.V.s used in medicine. Gordon designed and made the very first I.V. equipment that now is widely used in medicine. The Hoopers and their two children were steady members.

Doc Eckley

Doc was not a doctor, but somewhere in his past had earned this nickname. He was single, hard-working, and strange. We all loved him and he has earned a mention here because he was definitely unique. His skills were that he loved the Lord, the church, and was faithful.

The Congregation Grows

From the very first days it appeared that God had his special hand of blessing on the church because wonderful people came steadily into the church family. Here is a small list of a few of these fine people.

Mr. and Mrs. Dick Bussing

Dick was a pharmacist who worked for one of the major drug companies representing their products to doctors. He was a fun person, clean, devoted to Christ, and one who could be depended on to be faithful, wise, and helpful.

Midge, his wife, was a willowy and pretty lady, who was fun to be around and a wonderful mother to their two children. The Bussings took one of the three Navajo boys from the reservation into their home, and David BeGay was the very first Navajo baptized from the mission work that took place near the four corners of America. They had a significant part in his conversion and his long life of serving Christ on the Navajo reservation.

Mr. and Mrs. Ward Armstrong

Ward and Janine had six children and Ward worked in some technical capacity with Kennecott Copper. He was well educated and gifted, but also was a bit intractable in personality as described by Ruth Bender.

Janine was a super help in Sunday school, and their presence increased attendance and their generosity helped the church budget. They were and are fine people.

The Crawfords

Another of the early new families was Ron and Patti Crawford and their two children, Kenneth, and Karen. Ron was transferred in by his company where he was one of their top sales staff. Patti was affectionately known as "Pretty Patti" and this fit her well with her bubbly, warm, personality, and physical beauty.

Ron told me one day, "I am the only non-Mormon sales person of the twenty-person sales staff. At our annual sales meeting, that is held in Las Vegas, Nevada, I am the only one who does not have an overnight female guest (not their wives) in their hotel room." (This is mentioned because it gives a small insight into the rather lax view of human sexuality that I found in Salt Lake City.)

Ron's parents, George and Georgia Crawford, soon followed them to Utah and Georgia became the church's accountant and bookkeeper. They, too, were wonderful Christian people.

Mr. and Mrs. Paul Rees

A distinguished-appearing couple appeared at church and I had the delightful experience of visiting them in their home. They were Paul and Lucille Rees. Lucille was mature, beautiful, gracious, and possessed a southern gentility and charm. Paul had striking grey eyes that seemed to almost penetrate one's soul.

I soon learned that Paul was the number one boot salesman in America. He worked for the largest boot maker (Acme Boot) in America, and he was their number one salesman. He said to me one day, "Americans all need a good understanding and that is a pair of Acme boots." He presented me with a beautiful handmade pair of cowboy boots, that I still own, and sometimes still wear. I could have never afforded such an expensive pair of boots.

Paul drove the latest fine Cadillac car and sold more than twice the volume of boots as the second-runner-up sales person. He was asked to talk about what made his success possible at a meeting of sales people in Utah. A neighbor of ours, Larry Siglin, told me what Paul said and asked me what it meant.

Larry explained that Paul stood in front of the large crowd and explained his success by saying: "First of all, my success is because I am the most handsome man possible (he was bald, portly, but with striking grey eyes). I am smarter than anyone else anywhere, I drive a fine new Cadillac car and yes, I do sell wonderful boots." Then he said, "Seriously now, and I want all of you to listen to me as I am dead serious, I attribute all of my success to having yielded my life to Jesus Christ at the foot of His cross and He is the real reason for any success that I have ever achieved." With that he went and sat down.

Larry asked me, "Charles, what does it mean to yield your life to Jesus at the foot of His cross?" I then had the opportunity to explain to him what it meant to submit our lives to Christ and receive His salvation.

Paul sometimes would take me to lunch and would bless and encourage me with words of praise for my humble efforts at preaching. One day he took me to a fine clothing store and bought me a new suit, sport coat, shirt, tie, and shoes that I seriously needed.

When Paul retired, he and Lucille returned to his home town in Kansas and soon I was invited to come hold a revival meeting at their church. Paul said their preacher almost died from shock when he heard my first sermon and saw all the people who came to accept Christ and be baptized. (Probably the person most changed by this revival meeting was the preacher.) It was a wonderful revival there on the border of the Bible Belt. I can't wait to see Paul and Lucille in glory.

The Sloans
Vince and Arletta—Max and Betty

The first family of Sloans that came into the church was Max and Betty with their two children, David and Annette. They basked in the love and warmth of the church family fellowship, and the children found a home with the other Christian youth. They were so happy there that Max urged his older brother, when he retired, to move to Salt Lake City, which they did.

Vince had been an elder in a Bible Belt church and came as a strong blessing to the church as he understood how a successful church should be organized, and offered wise counsel to the church leadership.

David wanted to sing in the church choir, which he was permitted to do. Margaret said that some people sing on the white keys of the piano, and others sing on the black, but David sings in the cracks. At first there was a discordant sound in the choir from his singing. But with patience and training the last I heard was that David was singing solos in their church.

David went to Intermountain Bible College, became a successful business man, and elder, in the Colorado church where he and his family attend.

Mr. & Mrs. Leo Chenoweth

Early in the ministry in Utah, Leo, Ruth, Mark and Michelle Chenoweth became a part of the church family. Leo was chief technical/mechanical advisor for Wheeler Machinery and Caterpillar dealership.

Leo was soft spoken, clean, sharp, and devout. He loved machinery and took an interest in the cars I drove and especially when I bought the used 190 Diesel Mercedes. He provided diesel for this car the whole time I owned it.

Ruth pinning on a corsage.

Ruth had been orphaned as a small child in Germany, during World War II. She was adopted by a United States military family and ended up in Salt Lake City and married to Leo. She was beautiful and spoke with a slight German accent, which made her even more charming. She and Leo had been unable to have children themselves and so had adopted Mark and Michelle, both as babies.

Ruth was very active in the church and she was noted for her concern for anyone who was suffering or needed help. She was loved by the whole church. She made a beautiful cover for the communion table at the front of the sanctuary. It was deep purple with a gold fringe all around it.

Leo called me one day and he was crying so hard that I had difficulty understanding what he was saying. Finally he got hold of himself enough to sob out, "Ruth's dead!" "WHAT" I said, "She can't be!" But she was. She had the flu and had gone to the doctor who gave her a shot that he thought was an antibiotic but it was not and it killed her on the spot. She was just 32 years old.

I went with Leo to choose a burial plot at the graveyard and he stood shaking his fist at the sky and crying out, "God, why will you never let me be happy? Ruth was my life, you took my first wife, when she was only 24 years old with cancer, and now you

Adventures of a Young Preacher in Salt Lake City

have taken my Ruth." He sobbed and shook as I held him in my arms.

He then suffered guilt at what he had said to God. I explained to him that when in tragic grief, people often express their anguish to the one they trust most, sometimes speaking, or even striking out in anger. For you, Leo, this person was God. It was not a sinful attitude, nor sinful words, but an expression of your torn heart, and you cried out to the one you loved most, your Lord and Savior.

The whole church gathered around Leo. But what now was to be done with Mark and Michelle? The solution was that we took Mark and Michelle into our own home until sometime later when Leo married a lovely widow and the children could go back home. Mark is still alive and well and Michelle has since died.

Mr. & Mrs. Claude Killian

Claude, Geraldine, and their three children, came as transfers from a church in Portland, Oregon. Claude came to manage a Shakey's Pizza Parlor not far from the church building. They were mature Christians and had a lovely daughter and twin sons, Ellery and Emory. The Pizza parlor offered what was called "Bunch of Lunch" which was all one could eat for a very modest price.

Since they were members of the church, and had such a good deal for lunch, we often ate there. This gave us an insight into Geraldine's personality. One of their customers she called, "Little Jake." He was humongous in size and appetite. One day I observed him eating a whole large pizza, several bowls of salad, three large drinks, and 21 pieces of chicken. It was entertaining just to watch him eat. He would put a whole chicken leg in his mouth, twist it back and forth, and then swallow and repeat. (All for one low price!)

Little Jake's Buick sedan, sitting in the parking lot, sat lower on the front driver's side, due to his humongous size and weight. Geraldine would stand, watch him eat, and comment out loud, "Look at him eat, did you ever see such gluttony?" She was hoping to offend him so he would not return as he damaged their profit and loss statement. She never succeeded.

Geraldine's father had been Jewish and her mother a Christian. She had that Jewish shrewdness and forthrightness. She was often heard giving advice to me or some member, even Paul Rees.

Geraldine also played the piano for church on Sunday. She was a cute little thing, and we all loved her dearly. She and Claude won a trip to California by doing so well managing the Pizza Parlor. She was swimming in the surf and got caught by a huge wave and lost her dentures, both top and bottom.

I remember the Sunday well when she came in without her teeth. My goodness, what a change, I had to look twice to be sure it was her. Paul Rees had benefitted from some of her outspoken advice on a few occasions, and was heard to say to her that Sunday morning, "Well, my goodness, Geraldine, it is about time God defanged you." Those standing around, including me, got a big laugh out of Paul's wise observation at Geraldine's expense.

The Many Others

I could speak of the Pintuses, Kingleys, Andersons, Whislers, Roberts, Storys, Deckers, Bakers, Paulsens, Poes, ReCamps, Burkhalters, Acrees, Lessleys, Quicks, and hundreds of others. God had sent family after family of those hungry for the gospel and salvation. In seven years over seven hundred people walked the aisle to make the good confession, to be baptized, or to join the church family.

Yes, Pat McMullen had been used of God to nudge us out of the little Oregon church to a larger ministry God had us for. God bless you Brother Pat!

George O. Allsbury

When interviewing for the pulpit of the Christian Church in Salt Lake City, I met a man and we immediately bonded in brotherly friendship. This was an unlikely bond since he was a butcher and had only recently accepted Christ. George had been drinking a fifth of liquor each day and chain smoking when able for the past ten years. His life and marriage were a mess. He had decided to turn his life over to the Lord and was remarkably changed. He and his wife were among the about forty members of this small church plant.

Before making the move from Douglas County, Oregon, to Salt Lake City, Bob Thomas called with the bad news that George had been diagnosed with incurable lung cancer and been given only a few months to live.

Upon our arrival in SLC, George asked if I would mentor him in spiritual disciplines. I agreed to do this, and George and I began meeting together each Tuesday evening to work in discipleship and evangelism. The agenda was that as we drove I would teach him important things about the faith and the Bible. Together we taught people as we visited in their homes. Several families were led to Christ, but it was George who profited most.

Salt Lake City is a strange place to minister, since the LDS are so evangelistic they work on everyone who does not attend church. People will come to church in sort of self-defense to get rid of the LDS missionaries. This gave an opportunity to visit and teach these people.

Our visits were very productive and George gave his testimony how Jesus had taken him from a wasted life to joy in Jesus. George was like a sponge, soaking up the teaching as we drove from house to house and in our prayer time before I left him at his home later in the evening. We became dear friends.

It was a great sorrow for me to watch George, a young man of only 46 years of age, slowly die. After just five months he was no longer able to continue our discipleship sessions. He was soon in and out of the hospital and finally he was diagnosed as having just a few days of life left. I visited him in the hospital and we always prayed together.

It was Palm Sunday morning at 2 A.M. that the phone rang and it was the hospital calling to tell me that George could only live a couple more hours. I dressed and drove hurriedly down to the hospital to find George in a coma. I took hold of his hand and began to pray out loud for him. Suddenly he sat up and said, "Charles, how wonderful for you to come, I am just ready to pass over and be with our Lord Jesus. Is there anyone over there that I should greet for you?"

I replied, "Yes, George, my childhood and high school buddy, Herb Strubhar, was killed when he was 24. He was a fine godly young man, would you look him up and give him my love and assure him I will be along later."

To this George replied, "I sure will and I will be seeing you again." He fell back on the bed, took a few deep breaths and then quivered a bit and died. George in about six months had moved from being a failure at marriage, work and life. He had become a wonderful loving man of God. Though he entered the Lord's vineyard at the last hour of the day he received the same reward as those who served all day. My last words to George were, "I'll be seeing you, Brother George."

George Allsbury's Nephew

George had a nephew whose name was Sid Allsbury. He ministered to a small church in western Missouri. George had spoken favorably to Sid about me and not long after George's death Sid called and asked if I would come hold a revival at the church in Smithfield. It was on the Missouri-Oklahoma border, as far south and west as one could get in Missouri.

I replied that I would come if they would welcome a friend of mine to lead the singing and sing. This person was Roger Bankson. He was said to be America's foremost Irish tenor. I don't know about the Irish part, but he was the best tenor I ever heard. The meeting was to last ten days. Of course this is in the heart of the Bible Belt and people love revivals. I was not surprised to see the church fill up.

It was a small rural church that was planned to seat about 125-130 people. On the second night the place was packed. The people filled the sanctuary and the cry room. The deacons moved everything off the stage and set up chairs there. People were sitting with their feet so close to me I could not move around without stepping on someone's foot. Attendance ran well over 200 and continued to grow the whole ten days.

People came to accept Christ each evening and the church had no baptistery. We headed down to a small nearby river each evening to continue the service to sing and baptize people, with additional people coming at the river to also be baptized. Cars' headlights lit up the baptismal site. George, though now dead, still was having his influence for Christ.

The next year Roger and I returned for another revival and the results were similar with many baptisms and rededications. The church was packed each evening to overflowing. Yes, we traveled to the river over and over again.

Although the SLC church was primarily made up of young people and there were very few funerals, yet still all these years later every once in a while I still remember George and Lorene Allsbury and look forward to seeing them again before long. "See you soon, Brother George." George had a part in many others coming to Christ in Smithfield, Missouri.

A Neighboring Church

Another nearby New Testament church in Carl Junction, Missouri, asked me to come the third year for a revival and to bring my friend Roger Bankson. This was a larger church but they had heard about the small church revivals and some of their members had attended.

The meeting was off to a good start, and on Thursday evening at the conclusion of my message, it was clear the whole church was under conviction. It appeared to me that when we sang the invitation the Spirit of God would move many to repentance. (I learned later the church had serious internal problems which I had not known about.)

Just as I was ready for Roger to have the people stand and sing the invitation, the preacher jumped up, and hurrying to the front he began to exhort and harangue the people. He began to call out people by name and said Charles has been talking about you and your sins; you need to get up here right now and repent. He went on naming person after person and their sins for 20 minutes or so and the Spirit left the place and nothing happened when we finally did sing the invitation hymn.

We might as well have closed the meeting that evening because it was over. I went away realizing the church's problem was not primarily the people as it was their preacher.

Back in Salt Lake City

The Abels

The Salt Lake City church's banker, and also my personal banker, was named George Abel. He was tall, dark, handsome, and extremely well qualified for his position. As the church grew, so did the offerings and the church became one of his better accounts. Many of the members banked there. One could see the church from the bank building.

George was the "Stake President" of several LDS Wards. Each ward building had several congregations meeting in the same building. The ward buildings only seat about 250 people. The several wards, meeting in one building, were called a "Stake." He was quite influential in the area. He was a natural born leader that people respected and loved. I grew quite fond of George. He was charming and handsome. It was a pleasure to bank with him.

One day he asked if I would have lunch with him at the country club. I was happy to do so. When we were seated he began to share his testimony with me about his faith and how I might really upgrade my religious experience. He suggested that I read the Book of Mormon prayerfully and that God would give me a burning in my bosom that it was true. I told him I had read it and had some pretty serious questions about it.

I asked him if it were true that there were thousands of mistakes in the original Book of Mormon that had to be changed in order to make the book accurate. He assured me that this was not true. I asked if he could check it out and maybe we could have lunch together again soon and he could explain to me where this rumor came from. (I had a copy of the original Book of Mormon and knew there were about 4,000 changes between the original and the present one.)

When we met the next month for lunch he rather sheepishly said it was true, there had been many changes. He said this puzzled him. I asked him another question that day. "George, I have heard that the Doctrine and Covenants has really been drastically changed Is that true?" He said he would check it out and we could meet again for lunch in a couple of weeks.

When we met, he was almost angry about what he had found. He told me what I had already known, that the Book of Commandments, now called the Doctrine and Covenants, was drastically changed. He said, "Can you believe that doctrine after doctrine has been revised and some totally changed." He said, "Section one says these commands are from God and would never be changed and just four pages later they have taken out about half a page and these changes continue throughout the book."

This cooled our friendship for a few months and I felt badly that I may have been too bold with him. I was surprised when I received a call from him when I was out of Utah for a revival meeting in Idaho. When I got back to the motel where I was staying that evening after church, I received a message to call George, which I did. He asked me, "When are you coming home, Charles?" He said he and his wife wanted to meet me as soon as possible after I got home.

I met them at their home the following Tuesday evening at 7 P.M. and they were full of questions. I went through the plan of teaching that I had learned was effective in teaching LDS people, answering multiple questions along the way. At 2 A.M. the next morning we went to the church and the Abels were baptized.

I cautioned them to not be too vocal about their leaving the LDS church as there would be all sorts of social and possible economic pressures brought to bear on them. But the word soon got out that they were now members of that awful Christian Church where Charles Crane was the preacher. Things went along pretty good for several months with the Abels faithfully in church, sitting near the front each Sunday.

One day George came into my office and sat down and began to cry. He got control of himself and said, "I have been accused of robbing my bank." I asked, "Have you stolen anything?" He replied, "Of course not!" I asked him to explain and he did.

Here is the story in brief. His bank was Mormon owned and the bank had transferred a new man to his staff not long after the word was out that he had become a Christian. This man was planted to find a way to deal with this traitor to the LDS cause. After about a year he accused George of stealing from the bank. His evidence was about $321 of teller shortages and also that George had also been paying a person to clean the bank.

George was fired from the bank for embezzlement of bank funds, and he had to spend about $5,000 for attorney fees to defend himself in court. The result of the trial was that the man, planted in the bank, was convicted of perjury and fined and put on probation.

George was exonerated, but still unemployed, as the Mormon bank refused him continued employment. He could not get a job in Utah and had to move to California to find work. I met with him one year later and his black hair had turned white grey and he was still struggling to overcome the financial disaster brought on them because he had the nerve to leave the LDS church. The Abels became faithful members of a Bible teaching church in Southern California.

A Strange Phone Call at the Office

I was busy working away on Sunday's sermon when the call came. A young lady said, "My name is Julie and I have been told you are the person who can help me and my boyfriend Jarrod with some theological questions." I asked how I could help them and she explained that she was Christian and Jarrod LDS and they were very fond of each other except when they talked about religion.

Jarrod was a returned LDS missionary and was now playing football for the University of Utah. She also was a student at the University. We agreed to meet that evening.

When I met them I was impressed by how beautiful she was and how handsome Jarrod was. They both were very pleasant and I questioned them about their lives and families. Jarrod told me that his father traveled America debating Protestant preachers about the LDS religion. He had convinced other preachers so that they would declare that they accepted the Mormon religion as another valid Christian religion.

We Began with Looking at the Bible

I began talking about why I knew the Bible was accurate and unchanged. I showed them manuscript evidence to prove that the Old and New Testaments were unchanged. I then got out my Book of Mormon and Doctrine and Covenants. I also got out my photo copies of both of the original books.

The Book of Mormon

I showed them that the Book of Mormon had about 4,000 changes from original until the present edition. This amounted to about seven mistakes on each side of each page from the original to present edition.

The Doctrine and Covenants

I compared the modern Doctrine and Covenants with the original photocopy edition I had. Section one says on page six in verse seven:

> Search these commandments, for they are true and faithful, and the prophecies and promises which are in them, shall all be fulfilled. What I the Lord have spoken, I have spoken, and I excuse not myself, and though the heavens and the earth pass away, my word shall not pass away, but shall all be fulfilled, whether by mine own voice, or by the voice of my servants, it is the same: For behold, and lo, the Lord is God, and the Spirit beareth record, and the record is true, and the truth abideth forever and ever: Amen." (Section 1:7)

It sounds great, but on page 11 half of the page has been removed from the text and the book is a mess of deletions and additions throughout. There are 21 doctrinal reversals and even a letter, purporting to be from John the Apostle, has deletions and rather involved additions. After pointing these things out to the young couple I could see Jarrod was seriously impacted. He had received almost more than he could handle.

I suggested we conclude our study that evening and reconvene the next week at the same time. They agreed and when they returned I got out my Book of Mormon for an examination of some of its teachings.

I asked Jarrod if he had read and studied the Book of Mormon and he replied that he had. I suggested we look at I and

II Nephi. It begins in 600 B.C. with the destruction of Jerusalem by Nebuchadnezzar and his taking the Jews into Babylonian Captivity. The Book of Mormon affirms that 15–18 Jews escaped and after months of travel ended up in the Americas, somewhere in North, Central or South America. Joseph Smith indicated it was in North America somewhere near New York State.

Taking up the story in II Nephi the people enter into conflict and are divided into two groups, the Lamanites and the Nephites. In the footnotes in II Nephi chapter five it indicates that about 12–30 years have passed. The Nephites were the good people and Lamanites the bad. The Nephites consist of 4 or 5 men and boys and two women, possibly Nephi's sisters and possibly two or three wives.

Taking up the story in II Nephi 5:6,

"Wherefore, it came to pass that I, Nephi, did take my family and also Zoram and his family and Sam, and his family, and Jacob and Joseph my younger brethren, and also my sisters, and all those who would go with me."

Remember that there were only 15–18 that left Jerusalem and according to the footnote 12–30 years have passed. The point is that there were at best about 20 people with Nephi which is puzzling since only about 15–18 left Jerusalem about a dozen years before.

Now the story gets quite astounding:

V:13 "And it came to pass that we began to prosper exceedingly, and to multiply in the land."
V:14 "And I, Nephi, did take the sword of Laban, and after the manner of it did make many swords, lest by any means the people who were now called Lamanites should come upon us and destroy us; for I knew their hatred towards me and my children and those who were called my people."

What does it take to make swords in the wilderness? Iron ore, coal, sandstone, smelting, forming, grinding, and finishing. Oh, with a few men, a few boys and girls and 4 or 5 women, and while producing housing and food in the wilderness, they also found time to prospect for iron ore, open a coal mine and open up a sandstone pit. They had made themselves an iron smelter, forge and had made grindstones, and forms into which they could form the molten iron. Wow, they really were busy, I suggested to Jarrod and his sweetheart. Remember they have been in the wilderness about 12–30 years.

> V:15 "And I did teach my people to build buildings, and to work in all manner of wood, and of iron, and of copper, and of brass, and of steel, and of gold, and of silver, and of precious ores, which were in great abundance."

Incredible, they became master carpenters with all kinds of wood, had not only an iron ore mine, but a copper mine, were smelting brass, and even had a steel mill, also a gold mine, silver mine, and were producing all sorts of precious metals. These men and boys must have been pretty busy tending their gardens, hunting for meat to eat, and in their spare time prospecting and building blast furnaces to make steel.

Do you believe this yarn, I asked Jarrod and Julie? I see the look of puzzlement on Jarrod's face and know his faith in his religion is fading fast. I said to them, but wait, the best is yet to come.

> V:16, "And I, Nephi, did build a temple; and I did construct it after the manner of the temple of Solomon save it were not built of so many precious things, for they were not to be found upon the land, wherefore, it could not be built like unto Solomon's temple. But the manner of the construction was like unto the temple of Solomon; and the workmanship thereof was exceeding fine."

More rather difficult questions come to mind, Jarrod:
a) In one verse the construction materials that were in

Solomon's Temple are in great abundance and in the very next they cannot be found.

b) Solomon's temple took 170,000 men seven years to build, and here Nephi does something similar in the wilderness, while caring for his family, housing, feeding, leading, and at the same time mining, smelting, and building. Jarrod, are you buying into all of this story about Nephi?

c) What about the steel mill? This is a major problem since steel was not discovered until the 19th Century. There was no technology available to Nephi to have done this. Whoops, something doesn't add up, Jarrod.

d) Solomon's Temple cost billions of dollars. But no big deal for Nephi and his crew of 4 or 5 men and a few boys, really?

V:18, "And it came to pass that they would that I should be their king. But I, Nephi, was desirous that they should have no king; nevertheless, I did for them according to that which was in my power."

King over what and whom?

a) King over 10 or 12 people, some children and maybe some babies.

b) Nephi isn't too busy to take on another task besides temple building, smelter operation, mine oversight, and of course his sword factory. Quite a story, but it is not finished yet.

V:21–23 "And he had caused the cursing to come upon them, yea, even a sore cursing, because of their iniquity. For behold, they had hardened their hearts against him, that they had become like unto a flint; wherefore, as they were white, and exceeding fair and delightsome, that they might not be enticing unto my people the Lord God did cause a skin of blackness to come upon them. And thus saith the Lord God: I will cause that they shall be loathsome unto thy people, save they shall repent of their iniquities."

Black skin a sign of wickedness?

    a) Hard hearts cause black skin?

    b) Black skin makes one loathsome?

    c) Fair skin makes one delightsome?

That is just one chapter in the Book of Mormon. There are other passages, Jarrod, that are similarly filled with things that make we wonder how anyone with their mind engaged can read this and end up with a "burning in their bosom that it is true."

    A few other questions that might interest you, Jarrod:
    a) Why does the Book of Mormon, that was written from 600 B.C. to 421 A.D., quote from the 1850 A.D. Edition King James Bible, with the exact verses, chapters, and punctuation? Where did these old prophets get the often revised KJV?

    b) Is the account of Cowboy Snakes in the Book of Ether believable? Did snakes round up all the cattle and herd them southward and deprive the people of meat, except snake bitten bloating and dying cattle? Ether 9:26-34.

    c) Why does the Book of Mormon say David and Solomon were grievous sinners because they had more than one wife, while the Doctrine and Covenants say God gave them all these wives?

    d) Why do the Book of Mormon and Doctrine and Covenants contradict each other about so many church doctrines?

The second evening came to a close with Jarrod and Julie leaving after I had prayed that they would find the truth and have the courage to accept it.

    Jarrod called a few days later and said he realized how he had been totally deceived, but his parents, Jack and Marge Dean, were angry with him for even questioning the doctrines of the true church. He wanted to know if I would go with him and Julie to visit with his folks.

At the Senior Dean's Home

As we entered the Dean home I could feel the tension and knew that it was not going to be a pleasant evening. Jack was a truly impressive looking man, tall, intelligent, sandy complexion, with bright blue eyes. Marge was what could be described as a beautiful and maximized lady. Each could easily have graced the cover of a national magazine. Both were as fine of appearing humans as could be found anywhere. Their home was equally impressive, clean, expensively decorated, and inviting.

After cordial introductions, I asked that we might begin with prayer. I asked that God help them know that I loved them and came as a messenger of truth and love.

After prayer I asked if I could cover the same information with them that I had with Julie and Jarrod. They agreed. I got out my Bible and summarized the facts supporting that the Old and New Testaments had not been revised and the Hebrew Dead Sea Scrolls, and about 5,000 old Greek New Testament manuscripts, have proven that the claims that the Bible had been changed or revised were false and taught by people who were ill informed.

We then proceeded with an examination of the Book of Mormon and Doctrine and Covenants in a similar way as with Julie and Jarrod. At the end of the evening I could feel the uncertainty that the Deans were feeling. I timidly asked if I might return in a week to talk further with them.

This turned into a several week study that expanded into a discussion of other subjects and of the Mormon book, The Pearl of Great Price, and what has been found that proves that the

Book of Abraham in the Pearl of Great Price is clearly a fraud.

After weeks of study the whole Dean family realized they had been hoodwinked by cleverly-devised fables and a modern-day false prophet, Joseph Smith. They were baptized and they were freed from the bondage of this cultish system and found the true freedom in Jesus Christ alone.

Grandpa Sleeps in Church

A few weeks later a young family came to church and as usual I visited them in their home. Their names were Mr. and Mrs. Ronald (Janet) Rasmussen. I learned that the lady's grandpa was Spencer Kimball, one of the LDS Apostles. They were in the same Ward with him and told me this story.

They said, "Grandpa goes to sleep in church and snores. Another leader woke him up one Sunday and he came out of sleep swearing and taking God's name in vain." The Rasmussens said, "This has gotten us to thinking about the many things that have begun to bother us about what our church teaches. We really see Grandpa as a rather carnal person and not what we would consider as a godly Christian man. Could you help us understand what is going on in our family and church?"

I went through the teaching plan that I used to teach LDS people. Early in ministry in Salt Lake City I had learned that I needed to begin with teaching about why the Bible was true and had not been changed, stressing that Jesus is the savior for all mankind. The teaching of Joseph Smith was:

> "That hardly any passage in the Bible had survived as written, but has been drastically changed during the Dark Ages by the corrupt church."

I showed them how this statement was untrue and that the Bible has remained remarkably unchanged.

When I had shown how accurate and dependable our Bible is, I then showed them the 4,000 mistakes in the Book of Mormon.

Joseph Smith said, "The Book of Mormon is the most correct book on earth." In reality there are an average of seven corrections on each side of each page between the original and the modern Book of Mormon. I showed them my original edition of the Book of Mormon.

I then showed them my original copy of the Book of Commandments that is now called The Doctrine and Covenants. It claims to be the words of God that will never change on page seven and on page eleven drastic changes are made and this carries on throughout the rest of the book. I showed them that there are 2,786 changes, with over twenty doctrinal reversals. I suggested that there is not a more corrupted text of supposed scripture in existence than the modern Doctrine and Covenants. It still needs many more major changes to make it credible.

After a few more evenings of study with them, the husband, wife and children were all baptized and became very faithful members of the church family. This became widely known and accelerated the LDS church's dislike of me and increased the resistance to our ministry.

Invited to Have Breakfast with the Prophet

In the 1960s, Ezra Taft Benson was Prophet of the LDS church. He had been Secretary of Agriculture, as a part of President Dwight Eisenhower's cabinet, and after finishing that work returned to Salt Lake City to take the top position as Prophet of the LDS church.

I do not know for certain just why I received this invitation to come to the Hotel Utah, where the President resided on the top floor, for breakfast with him. It probably had something to do with several fairly well known Mormon people becoming Christians and leaving the LDS church behind. Two of these converts were from the LDS Apostle's families.

I was invited along with a few other Evangelical leaders, of whom there were only a few, and when we gathered I was seated next to Prophet Benson.

I have never liked to arrive late for anything, but especially when meeting with important and busy people. That morning I had worried about where I would be able to park, and how long it would take to find where I was supposed to go, so I arrived early.

I was sitting in the hotel lobby 45 minutes early for the assigned time to meet. I was just waiting there when a beautiful young lady, probably about 28-30 years old, came up and sat down next to me and begin to visit. After about 5 minutes she asked, "Do you like to play games?"

I replied, "Not really, as I am usually very busy, but my wife does get me to play some board games with her."

Adventures of a Young Preacher in Salt Lake City

She said, "The type of games I am talking about almost all men love to play. If you will come up to my bedroom I will show you the type of game I am talking about." Suddenly it dawned on me, this rather sheltered, farm-boy preacher was being propositioned for sex with her.

I was not only being solicited for sex, but in the lobby of the LDS-owned hotel, as I waited for a meeting with the Prophet. This left me quite nervous and puzzled.

As I look back on this event there may have been a subtle reason beyond the obvious for her soliciting me for sex. There was probably someone with a camera waiting. If the church could get this type of action out of me they would then control me and be able to shut me up. Or it may have been just a routine thing that happened in this hotel that was only about six blocks from the West's most prolific red light district, near downtown Salt Lake City.

At breakfast I ended up sitting next to Prophet/President Benson. He was cordial, warm, and a welcoming person that soon set me at ease. He began to explain that his purpose was to welcome us to Utah and that he wanted us to know the church wanted to minister to us and with us.

I was surprised by his rather limited and canned testimony to us. He explained that if we would read the Book of Mormon and pray over this reading God would give us a testimony of its truth with a burning in the bosom. I was surprised that at this level he would suggest such a subjective approach to conversion to the LDS religion.

I questioned him some and found that he was not well read in theology and in general not much more knowledgeable than some of the church leaders with whom I had been meeting. It appeared that inadequate church leadership reached clear to the top position in the LDS church. I didn't have the nerve to tell him I was solicited by a prostitute in the church-owned hotel lobby that very morning.

When I recounted the "burning in the bosom" idea to Dr. Carter Bishop, a physician in our church, he said, "When they tell me about their burning in the bosom I suggest I would be glad to prescribe a good anti-acid that should clear it up."

I concluded, after this meeting with President Ezra Taft Benson, that ignorance of their church started at the top and ran down to the average member. When anyone really began to carefully check out their teachings, scriptures, and history, they would soon be on their way out of this modern day cult and perversion of authentic Christianity.

Another LDS Apostle's Children

As previously mentioned, Ralph Hafer owned the largest independent truck and auto parts businesses west of the Mississippi River. This business was on Second West, near downtown Salt Lake City.

One of his employees was Steve Packer. Steve's father was Boyd Packer, one of the twelve LDS churches Apostles. Steve had noticed inconsistent teachings and behavior of church leaders that were not befitting godly people. He had begun to research the church's doctrines and had grown concerned that he and his family were involved in a cult, not authentic Christianity. He had observed what a fine and godly man his boss, Ralph Hafer, was. Ralph had witnessed to him of his faith.

Steve discussed his concerns with Ralph, whom Steve had learned to respect because of his godliness and honesty in business. This led to my studying with Steve and Linda, and their coming to know the real Jesus of the Bible, not some cultish view of Him.

Soon the Packers were regular members of the church and they found the freedom of true Christianity. Over the years they have remained faithful and as of this writing their son is the preacher of Southeast Christian Church in Salt Lake City, Utah. I was called two weeks ago and asked if I could come to SLC to participate in Steve's funeral as he had just died. He had served for years as an elder and one of the key leaders in the Christian church there.

Sure Would Love to Do That!

While still back in Douglas County, Oregon, a local preacher had taken a trip to Israel and the Middle East, and invited all the preachers of the area to come see the slides he had taken.

I had been fascinated with the Middle East since the third grade after finding a book with large pictures of the Pyramids of Giza. I had dreamed of someday going there.

That evening when I got home from seeing his slides, I told my wife, Margaret, that I just had to figure out a way to go to Israel. She said, "Better not plan on going without me or when you come home I won't be here." My reply was that it made the dream doubly impossible. So I laid the thought to rest, thinking it would never be possible, since we actually lived on the edge of poverty.

Now forward to Salt Lake City and our ministry there. I was asked to serve on the Board of Intermountain Church Planters, a Denver group of preachers who joined together to plant New Testament churches in the Intermountain West. There I met a brother preacher whose name was Talmage Pace.

One day we were visiting and he said he had just returned from Israel. My question to him was, "How could you afford to go, Talmage?" He explained that if I organized a tour group to go and if I got enough people to go with me, then Margaret and I might be able to go without charge, being the organizers of the tour, and doing all the work of leading the tour.

This was how we began to lead these tours in 1972 and have continued to lead these tours for about fifty years. Now to the reason I have brought this subject up.

Tour Leader David

On the very first tour to Israel, our guide was named David. He was an Arab man and I suspected he was Muslim. After a couple of days it became apparent he was a Christian. I asked him, "David, could you explain to our group how you became a Christian?" He said, "Let's stop and get some cold drinks and I will explain this to the group."

We were in the Arab section of old Jerusalem and went into a small place where we could all sit as David told his story. This was in 1972, not long after the Six-Day War. Remember that this was when Israel was attacked by 125,000,000 Arabs and Israel was at that time 3,000,000. This was the exact same ratio as when Gideon defeated the Palestinians in the days of the Judges.

David said, "Unfortunately, my wife and three children were visiting family in Damascus when the war broke out. For the next three years I could not find out if they were dead or alive. I prayed towards Mecca four times a day seeking their return, without so much as a hint that they were dead or alive. One day while leading a group of Christians from America, I was so distraught I could just barely go on."

"The tour leader from America noticed my despair, and asked the reason. I explained to him my plight. He said, 'David, you are not talking to the right source for help. Go home tonight and get on your knees, by your bed, and ask Jehovah God in the name of Jesus Christ for the return of your family.'"

"This I did and I was contacted the very next morning by the Red Cross with information about my family and later that week we were reunited. I learned that Allah is dead or asleep, Jesus is listening. We are all now Christians with a Savior who cares and listens."

Tour Leader Ned

On our next Bible lands tour we not only visited Israel, but included Greece and Turkey. Having gained a bit of confidence from dealing with David, I approached our guide, Ned, and asked if I could talk to him about the Lord Jesus Christ. He immediately looked worried, looking back and forth to see who was listening, and said he could only talk to me in a private place about Jesus. I made the opportunity for him to come to our hotel and to my room.

This hotel was named the "Otelle Ephesus Diana" at Smyrna that had a big statue of Diana in the lobby. She was huge, maybe twelve feet tall, and had twenty-four breasts. She was supposedly like the large statue of Diana that was in the pagan temple at Ephesus.

When Ned came to my room we went out and sat on the balcony overlooking the huge bay. I opened the scriptures and explained to him about all the prophecies that were in the Old Testament about Jesus and how He had fulfilled every one of them, hundreds. Of these 500 Old Testament prophecies, 353 were quoted in the New Testament. Jesus had not only fulfilled a few, but every last one of the 500. This was impossible unless He was who He claimed to be—the Messiah, and savior of all mankind. I explained that there was no other name under heaven wherein we must be saved.

I went on to explain that Jesus was crucified and resurrected with over 550 living witnesses to His death and resurrection, most of whom were still alive when Luke wrote the book of Acts. I explained that all other prophets were dead and the only empty tomb on earth was Jesus'. I said that a Christian does not ask directions about the hereafter at a dead man's tomb.

Ned said that he did believe what I had said but he could never be a Christian. If he did he would lose his job and his life would be in danger. He would be cut off from his wife, children and whole family. He said he just was not willing to make the sacrifice it would take to become a Christian. I have never seen Ned again. I do think about the difference between David and Ned and it still bothers me today.

Safwat Sadek

On a later Bible lands trip a friend, his wife, a daughter and one of her friends and I were in Luxor Egypt. These friends were Dr. Ed Westcott, his wife Carolyn, daughter Shirley, and friend Stacy. We had spent the day touring Luxor, Valley of the Kings, King Tut's tomb, the Temple of Hatshepsut, and the Valley of the Queens.

We arrived back at the airport just in time to catch our flight back to Cairo, and the next morning back to the United States. I knew it was critical for us to get back home because Dr. Westcott was to be performing surgery immediately upon our arrival back home.

When I went to check in our group, I was told our flight had been commandeered by the President of Egypt to be used for some government business. I asked when we would be able to catch a flight back to Cairo. I was informed that all flights were booked solid for the next 35 days.

Thinking creatively, I checked to see about passage on the train. It was booked for 45 days. I checked about renting a car to drive back. I was told there were no rental cars and the roads were impassable being blown full of sand. I checked about taking a cruise ship. These also had no openings.

I went back to the Westcotts and explained our plight. My comment to Ed was, "God has us here for a purpose let's see if we can find out what it is." The small airport terminal was packed with about 300 people, many just in off of the desert, and the odor gave a hint of where and how they lived.

I began to approach people, asking, "Do you speak English?" After asking many people and them shaking their heads no, I approached a man in a dark blue, pinstriped, three-piece suit, and he replied that yes he spoke English. I asked what our chances were of getting back to Cairo that day. He told me our chances were not good, but we would have to just wait and see what worked out.

I introduced myself to him, and gave him one of my business cards, and he introduced himself to me and gave me one of his cards. I learned that we were the same age and that he had a daughter and two sons, and I had a daughter and two sons. We compared notes and found they were about the same ages. I asked if he were a Christian and he replied no, that he was Muslim. I said, "Since we have nothing better to do could I explain to you why I am a Christian?"

He replied, "Yes, I would like that."

I had a small pocket Bible (that had belonged to my father Claude Crane) in my document case. We found a place in a corner of the room to sit and I went through the same teaching that I had with Ned the year before in Turkey. He listened intently and asked several questions as we proceeded. We continued this time of study for several hours.

At about 11 P.M. (our plane was to leave at 2 P.M.), an announcement was made that a large jet had landed that had missed its connection with another flight and there were about 200 seats available. Safwat said I should link arms with my friends and make a flying wedge and see if we could be in the 200 that made the flight. This we did and safely got on the flight back to Cairo.

When I finally found a seat, after feeling like we had been in a cattle stampede, lo and behold who was seated next to me but Safwat Sadek. We talked all the way back to Cairo.

When I returned home a letter was awaiting me from Safwat's daughter Azza, who had written on behalf of her father. He wanted to know what steps he was to take to become a Christian. It turned out that his wife was a Christian as well as his daughter, but he and his sons had not yet accepted Christ.

I replied, and sent Safwat a nice Bible with instructions for confession and baptism. This began what has been a long friendship and wonderful access to the Coptic Christian community in Egypt. I learned later that Safwat was an Egyptian Army General as well as widely known attorney.

On a subsequent tour of Israel I was sitting with some Arab men who had become Christians. Somehow Safwat's name came up and they said, "Safwat Sadek, he is one of the most famous attorneys in the Middle East." (Remind me to tell you more about him and his family.)

Church Building Is Too Small

Week after week people were responding to the gospel of Christ. The baptistery was constantly busy and soon the building was cramped for parking and seating. After prayer and a study of the needs of the growing church it was decided we needed more property and the building needed to be enlarged.

A lot next to the church was purchased and plans were drawn up for the expansion of the existing building that was now paid for. The plans called to double the sanctuary and classrooms areas. A local contractor was hired and the work begun.

The small house that had been the parsonage, that had the fire, was sold and moved away so the building could be extended. Money was raised to pay for the expansion and soon we had room to grow more.

How is that hooked onto your head?

One of the carpenters helping expand the church building was as bald as a bowling ball. The next day he came to work with a full head of hair and the other workers gave him a miserable time as I witnessed their humor.

One asked, "Did they sew it onto your head, or is it held on by glue?" Another chimed in, "They call those things rugs, don't they? Does that mean you fastened it on with carpet tacks?" Another chimed in "You know you could use some Velcro to hold it in place. That stuff has a sticky backing if you pull off the tape." He weathered the storm and did look better.

It reminds me of another rug wearer who was so vain that even his wife and daughters had never seen him without his wig. He even wore it to bed and locked the bathroom door when working with it so no one would know. Few people did, but then he became gravely ill and he made his wife promise that at all costs she would have his wig firmly in place when people saw him in his coffin.

The day of the funeral his hair looked very natural and no one would guess it was artificial except his wife and the mortician. She had made the funeral director promise that it would look just like real hair.

When she went in to settle up the bill, she asked how much extra she needed to add to the payment to take care of the extra effort on the hair. He said, "Forget it, five carpet tacks hardly cost anything."

The whole building project was a huge success and the capacity of the building was more than doubled. The contractor and wife became Christians in the process and were some of the very first to be baptized in the new baptistery. They became regular members of the church along with several others of their family.

A wedding in the newly-remodeled sanctuary.

Roy, Utah Church Plant

A young couple, Jerry and Ila Post, were trying to plant a church in Roy, Utah, when their car was struck by a railroad train and both of them were killed. We all grieved at this loss.

A man from the Bible study they were leading, Jerry Gurman, called me and requested that I come up and continue the Thursday evening Bible study. This I continued for a couple of years each week with a few more gathering as time passed. Several of these folks drove down to attend church at Southeast Christian Church each Sunday.

Murl Jones

Finally, an older preacher, Murl Jones, showed up at church and became a regular attender and very helpful to me as the young preacher. He asked to be involved in the Roy Bible study and took over the project. In a few weeks this led to the forming of a church there with the purchase of property with a house large enough for a meeting place for the new church.

Since Brother Jones was a full time employ of the Job Corps, leading a growing church was too much for him. In the meantime an associate minister, Neal Whittaker, had been hired to help at the home church.

Neal Whittaker

Neal wanted to become the preacher at the new Roy church. The elders saw the wisdom in this, and he took the lead and this grew into a thriving church. His wages continued to be paid by the home church until the church grew and they were able to pay him themselves. He led the church until he was called to another ministry in another state.

Neal is a man of impeccable character, love of the Lord, and good ministry skills. Our time together was productive and we had many interesting ministry experiences together. All of his ministries have been marked by integrity and sound Biblical doctrine.

Kay and Neal.

Under his and Murl Jones' ministries, the Roy church was placed on a firm foundation and remains a productive church today.

Harry Ropp

I was again invited to give a workshop on Mormonism at the North American Christian Convention. While there, a graduate student from Lincoln Christian Seminary came to me and expressed his desire to become a missionary to the LDS in Utah. He asked my advice and counsel as to how he should prepare for this work. I provided resources for his study to prepare him for this work.

When Harry graduated from Seminary, Neal had just resigned, and Harry was hired as the next preacher at the Roy church. He came and worked with vigor and soon was making a real impact for Christ among the LDS people. His Master's thesis was entitled, *Is Mormonism Christian?* This was published and soon became a hot selling book.

It was not long before Harry was known everywhere for his witness to the LDS community. He was being invited to speak all across America. He soon was widely known among the LDS church leaders and being vilified for his courageous stand for the gospel in contrast to Mormon dogma.

He and his associate minister were traveling in California to speak and stopped to have his airplane fueled where they stayed overnight. In the morning they continued their journey south. He checked the airplane thoroughly and paid for the fuel.

After being in the air about 20 minutes the airplane was out of fuel and stalled out while trying to land on a Los Angeles freeway. They almost made it over an overpass, but not quite, and the wheels caught on the overpass and they crashed head first into the freeway below. They were instantly killed.

Although it was not positively proven, Harry's father believed his airplane had been tampered with, and a fuel line disconnected so the fuel all pumped out of the tanks, leaving it out of fuel. It was a major loss for the LDS mission work and the Roy, Utah, church.

Each time Roy needed a preacher, Jerry Gurman would call and ask who they should hire next. I had recommended Neal Whittaker and then Harry Ropp. The next time Jerry called I recommended Dennis Whisler.

Dennis Whisler

One Sunday a new young man came into the building still dressed in his military uniform, as he had just been discharged from the Army. I'm not sure what possessed me, but my first words to him as he entered the church for the first time were, "God is calling you to the ministry of the Gospel." His response was, "Who me, I am a wicked sinner and smoke like a steam engine." He laughed at me, but did return to church and soon was baptized.

It was not long before he enrolled in Intermountain Bible College in Grand Junction, Colorado. He confessed later that it took him a few months to quit the cigarettes but he finally did. He proved to be a diligent student and completed his ministerial degree and was ordained to the preaching ministry.

In the process Dennis married Mary, a public school teacher, and together they ended up ministering to the church that was started in Roy, Utah. Dennis continued as the preacher there for many years until his retirement. The church was healthy and grew during all of those years of his and Mary's competent leadership.

Are Some of Our Members Polygamists?

Robert Thomas, the founder of the church in Salt Lake City where I was the preacher, was teaching Sunday school from Matthew 19 where Jesus is teaching about divorce. As a matter of comment Bob asked, "I wonder if we have any polygamists in our church family?" We all laughed and he said that would not likely ever happen. Neither he, nor I, knew everything that we should have known about the membership.

When we had moved in with Doris Monroe, she had introduced me to her neighbor and later told me he had three wives. The LDS church in its early history was full of polygamy.

Joseph Smith, the founder, had taught in the 132nd Section of one of their scriptures, The Doctrine and Covenants, that polygamy was binding on humans as a revelation to him from God. He said;

> "For behold, I reveal unto you a new and an everlasting covenant; and if ye abide not that covenant, then are ye damned: for no one can reject this covenant and be permitted to enter into my glory." Doctrine and Covenants 132:4

> "Go ye, therefore, and do the works of Abraham; enter ye into my law and ye shall be saved. But if ye enter not into my law ye cannot receive the promise of my Father, which he made unto Abraham. God commanded Abraham and Sarah gave Hagar to Abraham to wife. And why did she do

Adventures of a Young Preacher in Salt Lake City

it? Because this was the law and from Hagar sprang many people. This, therefore, was fulfilling, among other things the promises." Doctrine and Covenants 132:32–34

"David also received many wives and concubines, and also Solomon and Moses my servants, as also many others of my servants, from the beginning of creation until this time; and in nothing did they sin save in those things which they received not of me. David's wives and concubines were given unto him of me, by the hand of Nathan, my servant, and others of the prophets who had the keys of this power; and in none of these things did he sin against me …" Doctrine and Covenants 132:38–39

If you have further curiosity about this subject, you might read the whole of Section 132 of the Doctrine and Covenants. You might want to look at Jacob 2:24–27 in the Book of Mormon. Here it says David and Solomon were abominable before God because of their polygamy. The New Testament says no polygamy, the Book of Mormon says no and Joseph Smith tells us we cannot be saved if we reject it. Curious, isn't it.

The Ladies' Home Journal

Well, back to Salt Lake City. *The Ladies' Home Journal* had an article about this same time in which it affirmed that after careful research they had learned that there still were over 25,000 cases of polygamy in Utah. Polygamy was still wide spread in Utah.

It was not surprising that I learned from one of our members, a convert from Mormonism, that his sister was one of seven wives. I asked him if she was ugly, dumb or what? He said that he had met all seven of the women and all of them were quite attractive. He said one was a public school teacher, another was a CPA, and another one was a registered nurse, at a local hospital, and so on. He said all seemed to be pretty normal woman.

I thought that maybe we should be concerned that some of these LDS converts that were coming into the church might be still involved.

Carol the Polygamist

Along about that time a very lovely LDS mother of three beautiful children began to attend the church. I taught her and she was baptized. Her name was Carol and I will not give her last name to protect her privacy. She was very faithful coming to all weekly services, Sunday morning, evening, and Wednesday evening prayer and Bible Study.

Carol came one day with several boxes of books to give me which were most all of the general works of their church Prophets. This added to my growing LDS library. I tried to pay her for them but she refused to accept anything.

A few weeks later Carol suddenly quit coming to church. After the second week of her missing church I took my associate minister, Mike Lynch, and we went to visit her at her home. When we rang the bell she came to the door but stood so we could not see her. She said that we should not worry; she would be back in a short time when she was able.

Two weeks later Carol was back but wearing very big sun glasses that covered much of her face. But I noticed that what I could see of her face was bluish yellow. I surmised she must have fallen, or been hit by something in the face, but she insisted she was fine and didn't wish to talk about it.

A couple more months passed and one day I got a call from Carol's husband, Laman, and he asked me if I did any marriage counseling. I replied that I did but was not certified and had only limited training. He made an appointment and they came the next day.

My policy, at that time, was to talk to each of the couple separately and then together. I talked with Laman first, since he had called, and he was evasive and said Carol would have to tell me what was wrong.

I got Carol in alone with me and she also was very evasive. Both insisted that they loved each other.

Finally, with them together, I felt stymied and said, "You are not being candid with me and I cannot help you this way. You are not polygamists, are you?" Laman shook his head yes and Carol began to cry. It was like a dam breaking and this is what Carol said:

"Laman and I were married, I believing him a divorced man. But after being married a few weeks I learned he had two other wives with whom he continued to live. Being a Mormon, I came to sorrowfully accept the other two women. Over the past years we have had children and things have been somewhat peaceful."

"But now Laman has fallen in love with a fourth woman and wishes for us to be divorced so he can marry another woman. I have refused and now Laman has severely beaten me trying to get me to accept being one of four wives. I cannot do this now that I am a Christian and know how evil polygamy really is."

I said to Laman, "Are you committed to having multiple wives?" He replied, "Yes, my mind is made up and I will not change." I said to them, "It is against the laws of the land and of the New Testament Scriptures. Carol, yes, you are not in reality Laman's wife. Unless Laman will be committed to you alone, according to the laws of America, you do not have a marriage."

Seven Wives

Another of our members said his sister was one of seven wives. I asked him if his sister was ugly and he said that she was well educated and beautiful. I questioned him about the six other women and he said he had met them all and they were all attractive and productive. One was a school teacher, another was a nurse, another wife was an accountant and so on.

It is not uncommon to hear about people who are polygamists if living in Utah. We frequently heard such accounts.

And so Robert Thomas' fears were realized—Southeast Church had a polygamist member for many months. Polygamy is still widespread throughout Utah and in surrounding states.

A study of polygamy in the Bible will show that in every case it leads to seriously troubled relationship and families. God made Adam only one wife. Those of us who are married certainly know that one is the correct number.

Trouble in Zion

Raising children in Utah proved to be difficult. One afternoon, when it was about time for the children to come home from school, we received a phone call from the school office saying they could not find our daughter, Carol, anywhere.

We jumped into the car and quickly drove to the school. When we pulled up in front of the school, Carol came out of the big bushes in front of the school and came to the car crying.

When she got into the car she sobbed and said, "The teacher and everyone at school hate me." I replied, "That certainly cannot be true, let's go in and talk to the Principal."

When we got to the Principal's office, I told her what Carol had said about her teacher's words to her. She called the teacher to the office and told her what Carol had said about her. The teacher replied, "Some days I cannot stand any of these brats." We then realized there was some deeper problem, and after talking with the Principal and teacher we took Carol home.

At home I questioned her about what had been going on at school and this is the story she told us. School had been in session for about six weeks. Carol said on the first day of school the teacher asked every non-Mormon student to stand up. She was the only one of the about 30 students who stood up.

Some student yelled out, "Her dad is the preacher of that awful Christian Church down on Highland Drive!"

Carol replied, "Well my father is not a fornicator and drunkard like Joseph Smith was." This brought howls of protest from the teacher and students.

Adventures of a Young Preacher in Salt Lake City

I asked her how she had gotten the idea that Joseph Smith, the prophet, was a drunkard and she said, "I was reading about his death and he and his brother Hiram drank a bottle of whiskey just before he was shot at the Carthage jail in Missouri. He died with a belly full of alcohol, making him a drunk to me." She said, "The book also says Joseph Smith had at least 27 wives and the Bible says a church leader is to have only one." She was right on both counts.

Carol went on to explain that from that time on she was shunned by every student and the teacher treated her poorly. On the day when she was in the bushes, after recess she had tried to go back into the class room, and three boys held the doors so she could not get in. She had gone to another entrance door and the boys beat her there and held the door closed.

Finally when she was going to be pretty late to class she gave up since she knew the teacher would really be mad and further embarrass her before the class, so she had just hid in the bushes waiting until school would be over.

The sad part of all of this was that Carol was missing most all afternoon and the school knew it, but did not call us until time for school to get out. These kinds of things impacted our children as they were children of the man who kept baptizing LDS people. To this day Carol is one of the first to defend someone who is an outcast, since she knows how it feels.

Did You Really Say That?

I had worked hard on my sermon for several weeks and had it pretty well thought out, well, maybe all except the title. Knowing that the first named gift of the Holy Spirit given in Philippians 4:8 is "love" the message was to show that the church family needs to work hard at making the church a place of loving harmony.

My scripture text was taken from I Corinthians 13, which is known as the love chapter, and possibly one of the five most important chapters in the whole Bible.

All of this was well and good, but the first words out of my mouth sort of threw everything into a time of embarrassment. My words were, "I don't get enough love." What made this especially bad was that my wife, Margaret, was sitting in plain view of the whole audience, on the stage, next to the church organ that she played for the services. As you may not know she is very blonde and can blush furiously.

At my words, she blushed red-faced, and it was quite apparent that she was a bit put off by my telling the whole congregation such sensitive information. Of course I was not thinking of my relationship with her. I hastily tried to explain, as the audience roared with laughter, that none of us suffers from getting too much love. The more I sought to explain the deeper I got into trouble. Finally in despair I reverted to preaching what was probably a pretty good sermon. At least some people still remind me about it more than fifty years later.

When it was finally over, and the invitation song sung and benediction prayed, I took my place at the church doorway to greet the congregation out. Here came the five elders in a row and each gave me a big hug and kissed me on the cheek. Now it was my time to blush.

I wish I could say that this was the most embarrassing thing I ever said from the pulpit, but it wasn't. For those other blunders, you will have to ask Margaret.

The elders: Clyde Benton, Charles Crane, Tom Bender, Ralph Hafer, and Fred Getman. Ward Armstrong was out of town when this picture was taken—but was present for the love sermon.

Intermountain Bible College

Erskine Scates has already been mentioned, but now returns to the story when the subject of Intermountain Bible College comes up. Erskine and two of his friends were concerned that small communities all across the Intermountain West did not have good Christ-centered Bible-preaching churches. There were churches, but they were cultish, stagnant, or centered in their denominational dogma.

And so Erskine and his friends Earl Heald and John Ball, united to found a ministerial training school in Grand Junction, Colorado. Erskine was the superintendent of the public school system and Earl was a high school teacher, while John Ball was a local businessman. They were friends from the same church in Grand Junction.

Erskine's garage caught on fire, burning down with his car inside. The garage and car were insured and he reasoned that he could do without a garage and decided he would use the insurance payment as seed money to start a Christian college. He enlisted the help of his two friends, and together they bought a large house on one of the main streets of Grand Junction and organized what became Intermountain Bible College.

At the time there were about twenty-five small, weak, or dying churches throughout the larger area. These churches needed preachers but did not have enough funds to draw a preacher from these Eastern Bible Colleges and the Bible belt where churches were strong.

These three and several other men like Ed Shaw combined their efforts and enlisted the aid of their wives, Faith (Erskine's wife), Kay (Earl's wife), and Ruby (Ed's wife). These godly women provided support in helping start a Christian book store and in doing the necessary office and support staff work. Their children became the first students at the college.

The bookstore, under the wise leadership of Kay, became an influence for good all over the Western Slope of Colorado. It provided books for the students and became the book store for all of the Western Slope of Colorado and the profits went to help fund the college.

Soon the college began to attract young men and women from the Intermountain area to their classes, and the education the students received was probably superior to the public education available in the area under the wise direction of Erskine and Earl, who had been central in the public schools of Grand Junction.

A Board of Trustees was selected and their purpose was to give wise oversight, but more importantly to bring students and financial support to the college. These directors came from several surrounding states. I was one of the Board of Trustees for six-and-a-half years.

Erskine Scates and other professors from the college helped area churches and they came to Salt Lake City to assist Bob and Toni Thomas in founding the non-denominational Christian church there.

There were quite a few denominational churches in Utah, most of which were sort of outposts, but not thriving churches. Southeast Christian Church was the first nondenominational Christian Church within 250-300 miles. This meant that close brotherly contact with other like-minded preachers was a precious commodity.

Recently, my dear father, Claude Carl Crane, had passed away and I felt lonely and lacking in fellowship and guidance. My godly father had been my rock and confidant, and when he died there was a huge loss. Erskine stepped in and became like a father to me over the years of ministry there and this relationship continued until his death.

Years later, a birthday celebration was held for Erskine, and at that time we talked about the fruit of his ministry through Intermountain Bible College. He told me that when they began IBC there were 25 nondenominational Christian Churches in the whole Intermountain area, and that a recent survey identified that now there were 125 churches and that most were healthy and growing. He reported that there were preachers/missionaries around the world who had graduated from IBC. He told about the graduates that served in Africa, Europe, Brazil, and of course preachers that were spread across America who had gotten their educational start at this small Christian college.

John Ball, the local business man, was a truly unique individual. He gave wise counsel and generous gifts to assist the college. He was on the Board of Trustees all of its years in existence. He was bright and cheerful and had an almost crazy sense of humor.

John said he learned that a local man had butchered his mule for meat. He headed right over there and bought a few pounds of steak. He knew a well- known Eastern United States church leader was coming to stay at his home to speak at their church, and yes, he served him "jackass" steaks for dinner. I can well imagine the foolish grin on John's face after dinner when he asked this man, "Well how did you like that jackass steak?"

John told me of another occasion when he knew another church leader from Illinois was to be at their church and at his house for dinner on Sunday. He noticed that the tree in their front yard was full of blackbirds. He crept into his gun cabinet and got out his double barrel shotgun and loaded it. He slipped out the side door and blasted away firing both barrels at once. He said it almost knocked him down and did bruise his shoulder, but under the tree were a slew of dead blackbirds. He enlisted his wife's help and they plucked and cleaned a stack of blackbirds.

He said they were up about half the night getting them ready for his wife to make into blackbird pies. He said it really wasn't too bad, if you didn't know the source. Yes, this famous preacher ate blackbird pie and after dinner was asked, "How did you like that blackbird pie?"

Well, John and Louise invited me for dinner and I went with trepidation. I got Louise aside and asked, "What kind of meat are we really having?" She laughed and said, "John tried, but all he could find was T-bone steak, so you are safe. It was followed with a great cherry pie. I wondered if the cherries were from the tree in the front yard where John had shot the blackbirds.

IBC closed after Erskine, Earl, and John had passed on to glory. The new president was a fine godly preacher, but lacked good business skill, and the college was soon no longer able to meet its payroll and expenses. The college was disbanded, which was a great loss to the work of Christ throughout the Intermountain region.

Boise Bible College was able to acquire their excellent library, and some of the churches that had faithfully funded IBC now support the work of BBC. In reality Erskine's, Earl's, and John's investment carries on through BBC.

Ralph Hafer

Ralph Hafer has been often mentioned in previous chapters. It is important that who and what he was is properly recorded for history. He was one of the most incredible men I have ever known.

While interviewing to become the preacher in Salt Lake City, an old man (he seemed old to me a young man) came up to me and said he hoped I would accept the position and if I did he would become a member of the church and do what he could to help the church grow. We chatted for a few minutes and I gave little more thought to the conversation until much later.

One of the first families to respond to the invitation to become members of the church were the Hafers. Both of them were wonderful people, godly, committed and faithful. (Ralph's first wife, Mina, had died many years before and Margaret, a widow, was Ralph's second wife.)

Soon after our moving to SLC, he invited me to have lunch with him and to visit his place of business. The main business was called Hafer Truck Parts. Another of his companies was Spicer Transmission and four-wheel drive parts for pickups and large trucks.

The day I first visited, I was surprised to find over 90 people caring for customers all across the nation. I later learned that his business was the largest one of its kind west of the Mississippi River. It was a powerful engine of industry. But Ralph was a humble Christian man of impeccable character. We immediately became friends, almost as if I were an adopted son.

Adventures of a Young Preacher in Salt Lake City

One day he asked if it would be possible for him to travel with me when I went places to speak, hold revivals, or meet on Boards, and other church-related events. For six years we traveled all over the Intermountain West together. During these travels I learned a lot about this great man. Here is a little of what I learned.

When he was a child his parents were share-croppers in Iowa. Their source of water was a cistern that collected water from the roof of their small house. This house was provided by the owner of the farm. His mom and dad contacted typhoid fever from the bad water and both died, leaving Ralph and his older brother, Frank, alone, with no other known relatives. Ralph was 9 and his brother was 14 years old.

Since they no longer had a home, they decided to catch a ride on the train that ran close by the ranch and head west. They caught a ride on the train the next day and were on their way.

On the train were several hobos also catching a ride. His brother got into a scuffle with a hobo who pitched him off of the moving train and the train ran over him cutting him into two pieces, of course killing him immediately.

Ralph told me that at 9 years of age he had to borrow a shovel to bury his only known relative's remains which were grossly mangled and disfigured from being run over by the train.

After burying his brother, he was now alone, and so the next day caught another ride heading west on the train. He said that he was large for his age and had learned to work hard on the farm. He had finished the third grade. The only position he could find to provide for himself was working for Buffalo Bill Cody and his Wild West show as a roustabout. This he continued to do until he grew up.

He ended up in Idaho and learned that at Gooding there was some land available for homesteading. He applied for a homestead and was awarded a nice piece of land with the understanding that he had to prove up on it. This meant he had to build a house, cultivate land, plant crops and develop it into a working farm. When he had proven up on it he would then own it.

He told me he moved onto the land with only a tent and a few personal things. He set up his tent close to an irrigation canal for water for his personal use, and nearby he planted his first garden. He said he planted the first garden without any tools but his bare hands. He pulled the sage brush, worked up a small patch of dirt using a board as a shovel, and planted a garden for food.

After years of hard work he had a fairly prosperous farm, but made most of his income from buying broken farm machinery and selling used parts to the area farmers. During these years he married Mina and they had two daughters and a son.

Ralph told me that when he was about fifty years old he and the family were invited to an evangelistic meeting at the Christian Church in Gooding where he became convicted of his need to accept Christ as Lord. He and his family were baptized.

Ralph said a few weeks later he came into the living room and took out his pack of cigarettes and laid them on the mantle of the fireplace and said, "Lord, please deliver me from this filthy habit." A few months later the Camel cigarettes were still on the mantle and Mina asked if she could throw them into the fireplace. He consented and she did.

With his new-found faith they decided that they needed a larger challenge. They studied their options and decided to try to move to Salt Lake City. They listed their homestead farm and used parts business for sale. When it sold they were off to Salt Lake.

There they began to attend a Disciples of Christ Christian Church. He said his first act as a member was to give 50% of the proceeds of the sale of their farm to the church. He said for fifty years he had been robbing God by giving nothing and thought he needed to catch up.

With the balance, he purchased 20 acres near down town SLC on Second West and about 12th South. He said that a few weeks later the State Highway Department changed the route of the main North South highway to run right in front of his new property. His new property immediately became very valuable, as it was now prime business property. He said this was his first lesson that no one could out give God. He now had one of the best locations for his hoped for new business.

He began his business selling used truck and equipment parts. It was not long before they got the dealership to handle parts for the White truck manufacturers. With his acute business acumen and hard work this grew into one of the largest suppliers of truck and auto parts of all kinds, both new and used, in the whole western United States.

They also were the supplier of Spicer parts for most four-wheel drive vehicles transfer cases and drive lines. They soon were manufacturing heavy duty four-wheel drive trucks which they called "Ibex." These heavy four-wheel drive trucks were used in all sorts of off road construction projects.

Imagine all this when his last year of school was the third grade and he had been orphaned at 9 years of age. He had started with nothing at all and now was one of the wealthiest men in western America. But that was still not what defined him as a man.

His outstanding characteristic was his Christian faith and faithfulness. He loved the Lord Jesus with his whole heart. He was steady, godly, warm, humble, affirming, and never missed Sunday school or church. He would often be heard to say, "The Church is the only thing on earth with a future to it." He believed and lived that.

His place of business was run on Christian principles. He was the first major business in western America to share the profits of the business with each employee, now known as profit-sharing. To work for Ralph Hafer meant that you would eventually become a millionaire and most likely also become a Christian.

One of his hobbies was playing the stock market. He especially liked to follow the "penny market" in SLC. Not long after I became the preacher he had a pretty bad car wreck. I went to visit him at his home and he had broken one of his legs pretty badly.

This forced him to sit in his recliner chair for three weeks. As we visited together I asked him if he was bored just sitting there. He replied, "Oh, no, I play the stock market and I have made $350,000 so far."

Can you imagine what a great part he had in the work and ministry of the church in Salt Lake City? He was very wise about his giving to the church to be sure that the rest of the congregation also did their part.

During the hundreds of hours that we traveled together over the western United States he taught me so many helpful things. An often made comment was, "The Church of Christ is the only thing on earth with a future to it." I asked him to explain this idea and he offered so much wisdom on the subject.

He often said, "It takes wind to fly a kite." I asked him what this oft-repeated phrase meant. He explained that without wind a person could run their legs off and not get the kite to stay in the air. He said that any business needs wind to survive, for business the wind is good advertising.

He explained that for a church to grow it must have good advertising. The whole community needs to be told of the great things that are happening at the church. He suggested that our services needed to be advertised in the newspaper. He said we needed to cover every home with brochures about what was going on. He said that the church needed to be in a visible easily reached, central location. "It takes wind to fly a kite!"

He often said, "The three most important things in planting a church are location, location, and location. It must be visible and easily reached by lots of people."

Another of his bits of wisdom was, "Work is too hard to do to not have money working for you." I asked him to explain, which he did. He explained that all humans have limited ability and energy to work. A person gets tired and has to eat, sleep, and rest. But a good investment will work constantly 24 hours a day, 365 days a year. A good investment never takes time off. He advised about what he had learned about good investments and poor ones.

He encouraged me to find a way to earn a few extra dollars and then to not spend those funds, but to invest them. He explained that the cost of living was pretty well set for most families. This meant that from their income they had nothing left over to invest.

He said his hobby had been to see old broken cars, machinery, and tractors. He would buy them for almost nothing and then sell the good parts from them, and then would sell the scrap metal left over usually for more than he had paid for the whole thing originally. He said that the profit he made he would then invest.

He advised that an investment of $100 was like making $1500 since that was the overhead cost of living. He said he loved junk and this was his hobby, and it had provided the basis of his fortune. He advised me to find something fun to do that can make you a profit and invest that profit. It will soon expand your ability to bless your family, the church, and community.

A second hobby was the stock market. He especially liked the penny stock market since a very small investment might yield a large profit. One Sunday he came in and put an envelope in my inside suit pocket, saying, "Don't open that until you get home. When you have looked at it call me."

When I got home that Sunday after church, I found in the envelope a certificate for $300 of stock in Modern Mineral. It was for 3,000 shares. He said, "Just put it in safe keeping and I will advise when and what to do with it." Three months later he called and said to sell it. It sold for $3,000. I was then to repay his $300 which I did. He explained that was what having money work for you meant.

He explained that his very best investments had been in the church. He said that since he came to Christ he had never belonged to a church where he was not the largest donor to that church. He said, "Is it any wonder why God keeps showering me with great financial blessings?"

Few people have taught me more than Ralph Hafer, whose last year in formal education was the third grade. Be careful to listen to older folk, you can often receive a great blessing.

Many years later I received a phone call from Ralph. He said he was making some long-range plans and wanted to know if I would be willing to have his funeral when he died. I asked if he were ill and he said that he wasn't but just didn't like loose ends. I agreed that I would be honored to have a small part in such a memorial if I outlived him.

A few days later, the funeral plans arrived by mail along with a retainer check for $750. (A few weeks before I had borrowed $3,000, from the bank, to lead out by example, in funding an expansion of the church property.) The first payment was due that week.

I had just recently gotten out of Seminary and had spent our whole net worth on education. I had stepped out on faith to borrow money to give to set an example for the church. I had just prayed that God would help with the impending payment that was coming due. I cheerfully went to the bank and Ralph's retainer helped pay for the new land for the church expansion.

Four New Testament Christian Churches in Utah

While traveling with Ralph for me to speak at a men's camp at Como, Colorado, Ralph explained that he had been praying that before he died there would be three more churches like Southeast Christian Church. We talked about this and agreed that we would both begin praying about this.

The first of these churches has already been talked about earlier in this story. The Roy Christian Church was begun at Roy which is near Ogden, Utah, north of Salt Lake City. This church had its beginning by sending one of Southeast's members, Murl Jones, and a bit later Southeast staff member, Neal Whittaker, to lead in founding the church. Neal and Kay did a marvelous job in establishing this church that prospers still today.

A second church was begun in the West Valley by sending another staff member, Clyde Kelly, to be the preacher. Two elders and their families also participated in beginning this church. Clyde and Hazel Kelly were very godly people, and so dedicated to this new work.

A few months later, a third church was begun in Eastern Utah by several Christians driving there each Sunday to teach and preach the gospel. This made four Christ-centered, Bible-teaching churches in Utah. These churches each helped shine the gospel light into the darkness of an area of cultish false doctrine, and physical and financial bondage. Our prayers had been answered.

Dr. Max Ward Randall at the North American Christian Convention

The North American Christian Convention was one of the largest conventions of its type in America. When meeting in the Bible belt areas of America it was always thronged with people, but having it out West in Arizona and California provided more of a challenge since many people had to drive so many miles to attend.

In 1983, I was invited to lead another workshop on the LDS religion, which I did. The workshop was even better attended since the Mormon religion is so strong in the Southwestern United States. It was standing room only with many people who wanted to attend unable to get into the session.

One of the people in attendance was the well-known Missionary and Evangelist Dr. Max Ward Randall. Max had opened mission works on three continents and had been recruited to teach missions at Lincoln Christian Seminary in Lincoln, Illinois. At the close of my workshop he invited me to have lunch with him, which I gladly did.

(One of the drawing points of our leaving Oregon and moving to Utah was the promise that I could further my theological education in Utah. After arriving there I learned that my present theological education was as advanced, or more so, than anything available in Utah. So this idea had been laid to rest.)

(At lunch Dr. Randall said to me, "Charles, God is calling you to a much larger ministry than your present one. God has given you many talents and if further developed, your influence for Christ will be greatly enhanced. You need to right away go to Seminary.")

I felt honored that Dr. Randall had such confidence in me and told him that one of my unfilled goals for my life was to earn additional degrees to fill in the gaps in my usefulness.

Another brother, Dr. Wayne Shaw, at this same convention, also asked to have lunch with me and he gave an even stronger invitation to attend the Seminary where he was the Academic Dean.

Back in Salt Lake City

Soon after returning home, I received a phone call from Erskine Scates, President of Intermountain Bible College, saying that the Board of Directors of the college wanted me to be the next president of the college and a contract was being mailed to me. A few days later this contract arrived, and I placed it on the head board of my bed and prayed on my knees nightly about how to respond.

After a lot of prayer my conclusion was that with my Bachelor of Sacred Literature degree I was ill prepared to be president of a college. I traveled to Grand Junction and met with Erskine and he continued to encourage me to come lead the college. But finally I concluded that they needed someone more qualified than me.

After seven-and-one-half years of being on the front lines of this mission venture in Salt Lake City, I was physically, mentally and spiritually spent. I looked at my family and they were more and more bearing the marks of the oppression of the Mormon system on their lives.

Margaret and I were at the end of our useful service for Christ in Utah. Everywhere I turned I was on the defensive or offensive trying to stem the tide of the constant overbearing control of the LDS oppression. Although I loved the Mormon people more and more, I could not stand the thought of one more discussion, teaching session, or lecture on the subject.

I had another talk with Dr. Wayne Shaw and he said to me, "Charles, when you drive over the Wasatch Mountains heading east to Lincoln Christian Seminary you will feel like a saddle has been taken off of your back and the spurs away from your ribs." His words proved prophetically true.

Driving onto the campus at Lincoln Christian College and Seminary was like a preview of Heaven. It was an oasis for weary travelers on the gospel highway. It proved to be several years of warm fellowship, incredible instruction and renewal, and equipping for our lives ever since.

Looking Back and Ahead

The seven-and-a-half years in Utah were truly blessed by God. The establishment of a beachhead for the restoration of biblical Christianity in Utah still bears fruit. There were many hundreds of people who came to Christ, both LDS and non-LDS; with over 200 LDS people's baptisms, with them being freed from the bondage of a dominating cult.

Out of this ministry came several books:

1. *Do You Know What the Mormon Church Teaches?*
2. *Mormon Missionaries in Flight.*
3. *The Bible and Mormon Scriptures Compared.*
4. *Ashamed of Joseph.*
5. *Christianity and Mormonism, From Bondage to Freedom.*
6. A rewrite of Harry Ropp's book, *Is Mormonism Christian?*

Through these books, the ministry to the LDS people still goes on and several of these books are still in print and selling regularly.

The Church's Varied Influence

The church grew from 42 members to well over seven hundred. There were 254 baptisms and about 200 of these were LDS people. In addition, there were 462 transfers of membership, for a total of 716 additions to the church family in seven years. This does not take into account many who were baptized in revivals and summer camps. After one sermon, 46 high school age youth were baptized.

In the revivals in Kansas and Missouri, many people were baptized. On the Navajo reservations many hundreds were baptized. The church was heavily involved in the Navajo Christian Mission that literally changed the course of the Navajo Nation, turning so many of them to faith, Jesus, and eternal life.

The church's support of Intermountain Bible College, by giving lots of money, and sending many fine students, helped in extending the Kingdom throughout the Intermountain West and world-wide.

The church was a key member of the Intermountain Church Planters with several new churches being planted in Eastern Idaho, Colorado, and in Utah.

Yes, a young preacher in Utah, though only minimally qualified, was used of God for His glory, and thousands of people's good. Remember, God's son was a preacher. It certainly is one of the most beneficial of all professions.

The call needs to go out to our young men and women to give their lives to the ministry of the gospel. It is the only profession that has an eternal future to it. There is no more noble work than leading people to Jesus and eternal life.

Every Christian needs to do their part in promoting and proclaiming the good news that all of us were created for fellowship with God and to have life eternal.

The first day of heaven has been described as being as long as if a small sparrow came once every thousand years, and sharpened its beak on the Rock of Gibraltar, and when that rock was worn down to the size of a garden pea, that would be the first day of eternity.

As Ralph Hafer was often heard to say, "The Church of Christ is the only thing that has a lasting future to it." Be sure to do your part for it. Young man or young woman, won't you please consider giving your life to the gospel work. You will not regret it when you are old and when you face Jesus at the Judgment.

"For God so loved the world that He gave His only Son that whoever believes in him should not perish but have eternal life" (John 3:16). Jesus says to us, "I came that they may have life and have it abundantly" (John 10:10, ESV). —AMEN

Other Books by Dr. Charles A. Crane

1. *Do You Know What the Mormon Church Teaches?*
   (A brief comparison of Bible teaching and Mormon Doctrine)
2. *Mormon Missionaries in Flight*
   (Why a Mormon Missionary does not want to talk to a knowledgeable Christian)
3. *The Bible and Mormon Scriptures Compared*
   (A Text Critical comparison of the Bible and Mormon Scriptures)
4. *Ashamed of Joseph*
   (An accurate biography of Joseph Smith)
5. *Christianity and Mormonism, from Bondage to Freedom*
   (Christ brings freedom from Mormon bondage)
6. *Is Mormonism Christian?*
   (This is a rewrite of Harry Ropp's fine book after his untimely death.)
7. *Autobiography of Charles A. Crane*
8. *A Practical Guide to Soul Winning* (Discipleship)
   (Biblical management of the church for evangelism and growth)
9. *Personal Family Finance*
   (Becoming affluent with modest income)
10. *The Bible—The True and Reliable Word of God*
    (The result of fifty years of study of ancient Biblical manuscripts)

11. *The Families of Man, Biblically and Archaeologically Traced*
    (Humanity today can be traced back to Noah and the Ark)
12. *The Adventures of a Young Preacher*
    (A fun book showing the value of preachers)
13. *Irrefutable Proof that Jesus Is the Messiah.*
    (Three things that are positive proof we have a Savior)

www.ingramcontent.com/pod-product-compliance
Lightning Source LLC
LaVergne TN
LVHW051605070426
835507LV00021B/2773